"I wish I'd had Nicole O'Dell's *Hot Buttons Drug Edition* when I was raising children. It might have saved me a lot of heartache later. Bad choices can destroy a child's life, but preparation can protect a child from destructive mistakes. This book teaches parents how to prepare their children in practical ways. A must-read for every parent!"
—Terri Blackstock, author of *Intervention*,
Vicious Cycle, and *Downfall*

Hot Buttons Series

Hot Buttons Internet Edition
Hot Buttons Dating Edition
Hot Buttons Drug Edition
Hot Buttons Sexuality Edition

Releasing Spring 2013

Hot Buttons Bullying Edition
Hot Buttons Image Edition

HOT BUTTONS

DRUG EDITION

Nicole O'Dell

Kregel
Publications

Hot Buttons Drug Edition
Copyright © 2012 by Nicole O'Dell

Published by Kregel Publications, a division of Kregel, Inc., P.O. Box 2607, Grand Rapids, MI 49501.

The author and publisher are not engaged in rendering medical or psychological services, and this book is not intended as a guide to diagnose or treat medical or psychological problems. If medical, psychological, or other expert assistance is required by the reader, please seek the services of your own physician or certified counselor.

All Scripture quotations, unless otherwise indicated, are taken from the Holy Bible, New International Version®, NIV®. Copyright © 1973, 1978, 1984, 2011 by Biblica, Inc.™ Used by permission of Zondervan. All rights reserved worldwide. www.zondervan.com

Scripture quotations marked NASB are taken from the New American Standard Bible®. Copyright © 1960, 1962, 1963, 1968, 1971, 1972, 1973, 1975, 1977, 1995 by The Lockman Foundation. Used by permission. www.Lockman.org

Scripture quotations marked NLT are taken from the *Holy Bible*, New Living Translation, copyright © 1996, 2004, 2007 by Tyndale House Foundation. Used by permission of Tyndale House Publishers, Inc., Carol Stream, Illinois 60188. All rights reserved.

Library of Congress Cataloging-in-Publication Data
O'Dell, Nicole.
Hot buttons : drug edition / Nicole O'Dell.
    p.   cm. — (Hot buttons series)
Includes bibliographical references.
1. Parenting—Religious aspects—Christianity. 2. Child rearing—Religious aspects—Christianity. 3. Drug abuse—Religious aspects—Christianity. 4. Christian Teenagers—Substance use—Prevention. I. Title.
BV4529.O3433   2012   248.8'45—dc23   2012025295

ISBN 978-0-8254-4241-4

Printed in the United States of America
12 13 14 15 16 / 5 4 3 2 1

The Hot Buttons series, as a whole, is dedicated to my mom who had to deal with more hot buttons when I was a teen than she'd care to remember. Also to my six children who have so graciously provided the research I needed to write these books . . . whether I wanted them to or not. And to my husband, Wil, who somehow managed to make my teen years look like a walk in the park.

Hot Buttons Drug Edition *is dedicated to brave souls like Ed King and Betty Jacobson who have fought addiction and won, and then dedicated their lives to helping others battle its stronghold.*

Love you all!

➤➤➤ *The chains of habit are generally too small to be felt until they are too strong to be broken.*

—SAMUEL JOHNSON

Contents

Part Four: Parent-Teen Study Guide

Preface

I wonder if anyone has ever said, "You know what? I think I'd like to be a drug addict." I sincerely doubt that's ever happened. Addiction is born from a wrong choice made in response to a need of some kind—an emptiness that screams to be filled.

As a mom, I've strived to make sure that there was no emptiness in the hearts of my kids that would lead them down that road. I also vowed to find a way to make sure they didn't wonder about experiences so much that they just had to try them. The same is true in my ministry. So much of what I say has to do with helping teens find their value, acceptance, and completeness in Christ. When we look to anyone or anything else to meet the needs of our hearts, we will come up empty. The search to fill that hole will often lead down the path of addiction.

Years ago, when I was searching for ways to lead my children to make good decisions, I decided it would be far better to talk to them proactively about issues they would one day face than it would be to wait until they were buried under poor choices, like I was in my own teen years. I believed that if the information came from me, it would be easier to filter the information and help them process it in a healthy way. I wanted to find a way to help them see and understand the consequences of poor decisions without the added stress of peer pressure and other outside influences.

I knew I'd have to be willing to talk about the tough things like sex, drugs, alcohol, addictions, dating, and pornography, perhaps even before they actually knew what those things were; if I had any hope of being as proactive as I wanted to be, no subject could be off-limits and nothing could be ignored.

So I devised a game I called Scenarios.

I would give my kids a scenario as though it were a situation they were facing at the moment. It ended with a choice they had to make between three or four options that I spelled out to them. I made sure they felt safe in making any choice—even if it was clearly the wrong one. This was a learning exercise, and I much preferred that my kids make their mistakes around our dining room table instead of in someone's bedroom or in the backseat of a car.

The practice of Scenarios became a favorite activity in my home and proved invaluable in preparing my teens to make good choices. The best part was the talks we'd have after the choices were made and the consequences were presented. They felt free to explore, ask questions, experiment safely—and then, when similar scenarios came up in real life, they were prepared to make the right choices.

This book—and the entire Hot Buttons series—was birthed as a way for you, Mom and Dad, to bring those principles and practices into your home. You'll find each hot-button issue covered in detail, with warning signs and recommended action steps laid out in simple form. Then you'll find the Strategic Scenarios, which will enable you to approach your tweens and teens with these topics and give them the same opportunity to make safe discoveries that I gave my teens.

And I trust you'll see the same results I have.

Acknowledgments

I am thinking of three people very close to me who have overcome addictions in their adult lives. I'm proud to know them and so admire their strength and faith. I uphold them as examples of how addictions can be overcome in the strength of Almighty God. These three people stand out to me as miracles of hope . . .

My mother-in-law, Betty Jacobson, dealt with years of alcohol dependency before checking herself in for treatment and embracing the process with the power of God as wind in her sails. Since her recovery from alcohol addiction, Betty has been an AA leader and sponsor for others struggling with addiction.

My mom, Carolyn Charz, ended a thirty-year love affair with nicotine completely cold turkey. No patches, no gum—just resolve and prayer. She has never looked back and I'm so proud of her.

My husband, Wil, has overcome several kinds of addiction in his life. I have so much respect for the way he embraced the power of God to turn his life around. One such story involves his twenty-year smoking habit. One night he lay in his bed and prayed that God would take the addiction from him. He woke up the next morning without a bit of desire for a cigarette and never smoked again.

Those three people prove that it can be done through the power of Christ. Addiction is a stronghold, but our God is mighty and able to break the chains.

PART ONE

Drug HOT BUTTONS

What exactly is a hot-button issue? A hot button is any emotional or controversial issue that has the potential to trigger intense reaction. What topics jump to mind that fit this description when you think of teens and tweens? Pretty much everything that pummels your kids with temptation and threatens to pull them away from a walk with God. Music, dating, computer use, texting, partying . . . The list goes on. Moms and Dads, these issues are real and often confusing. They require attention—before they arise. Ignoring them can have dire consequences that our children will have to live with for the rest of their lives. The decision to just wait until an actual situation arises before we face a subject is naive, at best, and possibly lethal. We have both a parental right and a godly responsibility to hit these issues hard, head-on. If we approach them preemptively, our teens will be prepared to face and handle life's toughest battles.

Prepared:
Answering *Why*

When you hear the word *addiction*, what do you think of? Drugs? Alcohol? Cigarettes? They're all part of it, that's for sure. When we're talking about teens and addiction, though, it's more than the substance itself. We need to look at the whys, whens, hows, and wheres of anything that draws our teens in, captivates their attention, and places a stronghold on their hearts and minds as well as their bodies.

When teenagers cling to a substance or a habit as a means of release and grow dependent on it, it becomes paramount to everything else—including your wishes and God's will, not to mention friendships, goals, ambitions, and reputations. But what can you do?

> Your kids are going to experiment with things no matter what,
> > *aren't they?*
> All teenagers do,
> > *don't they?*
> And there's nothing you can do about it,
> > *right?*

You're powerless in the struggle against temptation and experimentation.

You should probably just pray hard, hold on, and hope the storm passes with little collateral damage.

A taste of alcohol now and then doesn't equal alcoholism, and puffing on a cigarette out behind the movie theater doesn't make someone a chain smoker.

Right?

Wrong.

Experiment is nothing but a soft word for sin and disobedience. It's a way to excuse poor choices as a sort of rite of passage and overlook behaviors that could have tragic, life-altering effects. We can't look the other way when it comes to anything our kids do, but that's even more true with behaviors that can lead to addiction, which is a powerful stronghold. Rest assured, we'll talk in great detail about the mechanics of teenage addiction in chapter 4, and you'll discover some surprising truths.

Dispel the myth of effective insulation.

When I was a teenager, things like alcohol, cigarettes, and drugs were never far from my thoughts or my friends' minds. I remember testing my parents' boundaries at wedding receptions, backyard barbecues, birthday parties, and any other events where I thought they might have their guard down.

I'd ask for a sip of their drink or even try to finagle my own at a wedding. I'd feign curiosity about their cocktail to get them to offer me a taste. And that was right in front of them; you can only imagine what was going on behind the scenes . . . sneaking alcohol from my dad's stash, buying cigarettes from the vending machine in the lobby at the Chinese restaurant. I never did illegal drugs, thankfully—but that was only by the grace of God because there wasn't a whole lot I said no to.

Through trial and error, I learned what I could get away with, and I came to understand how my parents really felt about those things. Although drinking and smoking were forbidden, since my parents smoked and drank alcohol to differing degrees themselves, I figured out that they wouldn't let me do it because I was underage, and thus it was illegal, not because they really saw anything inherently wrong with those things.

In other words, they told me not to drink or do drugs, but since we never really had discussions about why certain things were okay for them to do but not for me, I drew my own conclusions about what was okay and why. I took it as a "do as I say, not as I do" situation.

Parents, it's not enough to just say *no* or *don't*. You can't just turn your kids out into the world unarmed and unprepared for things they can't avoid. Our kids will face temptation, peer pressure, and sinful desires; it's a fact. Nothing we do can fully protect our kids from encountering pressure-filled moments where they're forced into decisions between right and wrong. You can't control what their peers throw at them, but you can affect how prepared they are to defend themselves against the onslaught. Our teens need to be equipped to make the right choice; armed with something more than *no*; braced by facts, your wisdom, and God's Word.

Take the mystery out of sin!

The early years are for training our children. In Mark 14:38, we're warned to watch and pray about temptation. The spirit might be willing to avoid it, but the body is weak. How much more so for someone who isn't prepared for the temptation? We may have raised the most well-intentioned kids on the planet. But even though their spirit is willing, their flesh is weak—they need to be trained and girded up with the strength to say no.

We ignore a huge need if we pretend we live in a Christian bubble while the world is crashing down around our teens. It's more important to prepare your children than it is to attempt to create a sterile environment in a world that makes that impossible.

> **Fix these words of mine in your hearts and minds**; tie them as symbols on your hands and bind them on your foreheads. **Teach them to your children**, talking about them when you sit at home and when you walk along the road, when you lie down and when you get up. (Deut. 11:18–19)

While you absolutely should have high expectations and maintain a tight grip on the reins as you raise your family, you also need to prepare your kids to face persecution, disappointment, and even out-and-out rejection when they choose to stand for what's right in the face of peer pressure. They need to be armed with the tools necessary to make hard choices. You can't just hand down rules and regulations, expecting your kids to follow them and then muddle through the fallout alone. They need to know what's coming. Your job is threefold: to help them figure out why they should care, to give them the tools they need to succeed, and to walk them step-by-step through the process of making good choices.

Why should they care? What's in it for your teens that will encourage them to stand in the face of peer pressure, risking friendships, popularity, and fun times?

- Are they aware of health concerns associated with addictions?
- Do they understand the legalities that go along with teenage drug and alcohol use?
- Do they fully grasp the realities of the stronghold of addiction?
- Do they see the value in keeping themselves free from the claws of sin?
- Do they value your wishes and seek to honor you as you lead them?

What do they need? Our teens and preteens need options. Wholesome things like church activities and sports, rather than too much time home alone riddled with boredom and mischief. But not so busy a life that they don't have time to really know you. They need to be a part of a family that is serving the Lord, and watching parents who practice what they preach. They need to continuously grow in the knowledge of the Word and in relationship with God.

How can they walk through this? Mom, Dad, Guardian, your kids need you to model a godly lifestyle in front of them. This might force you to ask yourself some tough questions when it comes to addictive behaviors or substances to figure out what kind of nonverbal message you're sending and to make sure it lines up with what you say.

Your teens need you to walk with them, hand in hand, step by step.

Prepared: Answering *Why*

They need you to be aware of what's going on in their hearts and minds and also in the lives of their friends. They need to know that you'll do whatever is needed to help them honor God, obey you, and respect themselves, including open the door to outside resources when necessary. All this requires time, communication, and godly insight. None of these things just happen; they come from intentional pursuit.

We can be confident parents, even in these scary times!

Today's choices have such far-reaching and permanent consequences for our kids, it's hard to trust that everything will just work out just fine in the end. Some of our teens' decisions will affect the rest of their lives. Knowing that they're ill-equipped to make those choices, it's very difficult not to panic. It would be easier to lock them up for a few years and check in at, oh, around twenty-two.

We do have a promise to cling to, though.

> **Being confident of this**, that he who began a good work in you **will carry it on to completion** until the day of Christ Jesus. (Phil. 1:6)

Let's break that down.

> *Being confident of this:* You can be sure that this is the way it is. It's a promise. God's Word is true and He follows through. You don't have to wonder if this promise will apply to you or to your kids. He said it; you can believe it.

He who began: Who began it? He did. Not you. Not your teen. Knowing that He made the first move toward your teen, and having the assurance He'll keep His Word takes a lot of the pressure off and releases the fear.

A good work: The work He started is a good and righteous thing. There's no doubt that He's operating with your teens' best interests at heart and that He'll follow through with the promise of the Blessed Hope of salvation in Christ Jesus, which is the ultimate good work.

Will carry it on to completion: It will be finished. He didn't start something only to see it fall to pieces because of some teenage mistakes. It will be completed. It's a promise of God that you can believe without a single shred of doubt.

Until the day of Christ Jesus: Here's the thing, though. Every one of us, including our teens, is a work in progress. This work, which will be completed, has a long way to go . . . until the day of Christ Jesus, to be exact.

When you see mistakes happen, when your teen seems to pull away, rest assured that the work was begun by God, and it will be completed by Him.

It's a promise.

CHECK POINTS

✓ *Experiment* is nothing but a soft word for sin and disobedience. It's a way to excuse poor choices as a sort of rite of passage and to overlook behaviors that could have tragic, life-altering effects. We can't look the other way with behaviors that can lead to addiction.

✓ Our kids will face temptation, peer pressure, and sinful desires; it's a fact. Nothing we do can fully protect our kids from encountering pressure-filled moments where they're forced into decisions between right and wrong.

✓ While you absolutely should have high expectations and maintain a tight grip on the reins as you raise your family, you also need to prepare your kids to face persecution, disappointment, and even out-and-out rejection when they choose to stand for what's right in the face of peer pressure.

✓ Your job is threefold: to help them figure out why they should care, to give them the tools they need to succeed, and to walk them step-by-step through the process of making good choices.

✓ Your kids need you to model a godly lifestyle in front of them.

✓ They need to know that you'll do whatever is needed to help them honor God, obey you, and respect themselves, including open the door to outside resources when necessary. All this requires time, communication, and godly insight. None of these things just happen; they come from intentional pursuit.

Watchful:
Answering *When*

These days, young people are forced to make adult decisions long before we think they'll have to and long before they're ready. Since we weren't expecting the issues to come up so soon, and our kids had no idea what was looming on their horizon, they inevitably make mistakes out of a plain and simple lack of foresight. We need to help them predetermine what their choice is going to be because they aren't mature enough to think clearly in the heat of the moment about an issue they haven't prepared for. At those times, it's far easier to just give in to peer pressure than it is to come up with the right alternative and be strong enough to live it out.

You have to be willing to tackle tough issues openly and honesty with your children before the pressure actually comes. That might feel uncomfortable—like you're giving your preteen or teenager too much information, too soon. That can be especially scary when it comes to enticements you know will be tempting. But you'll see, through the course of this and all of the Hot Buttons books, why the discomfort is necessary. Today's youth need to be trained in the actual words to say to turn down alcohol, brush away a cigarette, walk away from drugs—*long* before they actually have to do it.

Since the world is throwing temptation and sin at your kids at incredibly young ages—if you haven't heard them yet, you're never going to believe the statistics—you need to go after those tough issues even earlier than you think. If your daughter is going be tempted with alcohol in ninth grade, she needs to learn about the effects and the consequences and develop a plan for saying no while she's in seventh grade. If she's going to be pressured to smoke pot in tenth grade, teach her why and how to say no in eighth. If your son is going to be handed drugs at fourteen, teach him how to walk away far earlier than that. Assuming your teens will make it through those issues unscathed without preparation is like pushing them off a cliff hoping they'll learn to fly before they hit the ground.

If you ignore these things, you may find yourself having a completely different conversation with your teen. One about a real-life addiction, drunk driving, rehab, or even legal concerns. In that moment, as you have those tough talks laced with intense regret, you'll wish you could go back and do the hard prep work to save them from that error in judgment in the first place.

What don't your kids want you to know?

They don't want to admit that they're mentally exploring the ideas and possibilities that have to do with the things they're discovering about themselves and others. Your teens don't want you to know that they are attracted by sin, that they've considered disobedience, and that experimentation is a real possibility for them. They also would prefer you remain clueless about the actions of their friends. Why? Because they don't want you to interfere with their friendships, or to put two and two together and come up with *Uh-oh! My kid might do that too!*

Those first flirts with danger, the first tempting taste of alcohol or hit of pot—if all goes well—pave the way for more and more. The only way to prevent that is with information and awareness. Pretending it doesn't exist is like not talking about the elephant in the room; eventually, that elephant is going to get hungry. So it is with the enticements of sin.

How early is too early?

Can't I just wait until it becomes an issue? I get asked that question a lot. In fact, in its various forms, it ranks up there as one of the most common things I hear from parents.

Why bring things up early?

Wouldn't it push them toward the sin rather than shield them from it?

The teen years will fly by; maybe I can just wait it out and hope for the best.

I've heard that last one more than a few times, believe it or not. The fact that the teen years will fly by is exactly why it's vital that you not attempt to wait them out.

Waiting until your kids come face-to-face with life's temptations and tough issues and expecting them to know how to handle something they haven't prepared for . . . well, it doesn't make a bit of sense. Have you ever been hired for a job and been offered no training whatsoever, only to have been thrust into action and expected to do well? That would be the worst sort of management imaginable. You'd be set up for complete and abject failure. It's the same with parenting.

In case you still have doubt, let me ask you some questions:

- Do your kids laugh at TV shows that depict people drunk or high?
- Do your kids joke about alcohol, show interest in it, or pretend to be drunk or high?
- Do they go to any type of parties without you?
- Do your kids spend hours at home without parental supervision, such as while you're at work?
- Are there people your kids look up to who drink or smoke, such as relatives, coaches, or pop stars?
- Have they ever heard you say something like, "Man, I need a drink"?
- Have you ever caught your teen sipping or tasting an alcoholic beverage, smoking a cigarette, using drugs?
- Have you ever served it to them?
- Do you use any substances in your home?

If you answered yes to any of those questions, it may already be too late for the kind of preemptive strike I'm talking about, and you'll be doing a bit more of a reactive strike—which is equally necessary, but potentially more difficult. And, just to be clear, I'm not saying that all of those things in that checklist are in themselves bad things that doom your teen to a life of Alcoholics Anonymous. But we have to be realistic and admit that they are open doors exposing your kids to issues you need to address. Now.

How old is old enough?

Teaching kids the dangers of drugs and alcohol needs to start so much younger than teaching them the dangers of premarital sex. Unlike some topics of discussion, you can't wait for middle school or puberty, or even evidence of curiosity on the subject. Even if these substances aren't in your own home, they are in many of the homes your teens frequent, and when you add inhalants to the list, it's your home too! If your kids are old enough to go to friends' houses without you, you need to be having discussions about drugs of various kinds.

What don't you want your kids to know?

Oh, believe me, I could make a list a mile long of the things I wish my tweens and teens didn't know about, and I'm sure you feel the same way. The problem is, your kids *will* be aware of all those things, if they aren't already. Turn your thinking away from not wanting them to know *about* dangerous substances, and focus instead on not wanting them to get curious and *explore* the substances for themselves. It's vital that you're educated about what your kids are exposed to, armed with the tools to guide them, and then ready to take charge.

Regarding the substances that lead to addiction, you want them to understand but not experience:

> ➤ How it feels to be high
> ➤ How one mistake leads to another one
> ➤ The pain of the aftereffects
> ➤ The consequences—short and long term
> ➤ The desire to undo something that can't be erased
> ➤ Regret
> ➤ Addiction

Let's stop being horrified by the truth about what our teens are faced with and start doing something to equip them to handle it. This book deals with alcohol, cigarettes, street drugs, inhalants, and all of the various dangers that accompany those things. When you turn the heat up on this issue, you may see smoke in every direction, signaling there are already some fires smoldering in your home. It's okay, don't panic—but it's time to get serious. Remember: God is in control.

CHECK POINTS ➤➤➤

CHECK POINTS

✓ Today's youth need to be trained in the actual words to say to turn down alcohol, brush away a cigarette, walk away from drugs—*long* before they actually have to do it.

✓ Waiting until your kids come face-to-face with life's temptations and tough issues and expecting them to know how to handle something they haven't prepared for . . . well, it doesn't make a bit of sense.

✓ If your kids are old enough to attend sleepovers, whether you let them or not, you need to be having discussions about drugs of various kinds.

✓ Turn your thinking away from not wanting them to know about dangerous substances, and focus instead on not wanting them to get curious and explore the substances for themselves.

✓ Let's stop being horrified by the truth about what our teens are faced with and start doing something to equip them to handle it.

Proactive:
Answering *How*

If raising children were simple, parents would be able to share stories of their own mistakes and offer advice to their kids who would then accept and apply said advice without question. Parents would impart the wisdom they gleaned from their own personal failures and poor decisions, and the children would see their parents as interesting, protective, and wise. They would cling to the sage advice and suggestions their parents offered . . . in fact, they would beg for it.

In a fairy tale, maybe.

Every parent knows that's just not the way it works. We didn't treat our parents that way, and our kids won't see us in that light either. Most preteens will pretend to listen just long enough to make Mom and Dad happy, and then blissfully and confidently go their own way, shucking the parental words off their shoulders with each step while they proceed to do whatever they want.

Like you and I did.

If we can't just wait and let them figure it out in their own timing, and we can't just tell them the way it is and leave it at that, then we need to find another way to reach them. Young people learn best through personal experience, but we don't want to wait until they make the mistakes in order for them to learn from the issues. So, what can we do?

Whatever you do, don't relate.

No matter how hard you try, you're Mom or Dad—you'll never be cool. And that's a good thing. You may have moments where your teens think you're the greatest, but isn't that usually because they've gotten their way about something?

Instead of trying to relate to your teen as a contemporary, instead of turning a blind eye during a toast at a wedding or allowing them a drag of Uncle Morey's cigarette, gain credibility with them by standing firm. Even if they're frustrated or angry with you because everyone else's parents are so much cooler, deep down they're relieved . . . even if they don't realize it yet.

Your teens don't want you to be a drinking buddy, they want you to guide them toward safety. They certainly don't want you to look the other way while they embark on dangerous behaviors—they want you to set boundaries and teach them the way to walk. If they can't count on you to want the best for their long, healthy, and happy life, who can they count on?

You can't parent well if your focus is on maintaining the status of cool in your teens' eyes. In fact, they don't want you to fill the role of BFF; they want you to be the *parent*. Your kids get to choose from millions of potential friends in the world, but they only have access to a couple of parents.

What Not to Say

When you're talking to your teens and preteens about drugs (or anything, for that matter), avoid trying to use teen-speak. It robs you of your credibility. My daughter says *uber* and *epic* all the time, but if I joke around and throw one of those words into a sentence, she just rolls her eyes. Why? Because she knows it's not me and that I'm just desperately and pathetically trying to relate to her on a level where she doesn't need me or want me to be. It's fake and contrived. Teenagers see right through that every single time.

Along with skipping those uberly epic phrases (see what I mean?), you want to think before you relate. You want to be open and honest about your history, without sensationalizing it. Don't tell your stories with a back-in-the-day feel, but definitely don't shy away from your kids' questions and curiosity about you. These are defining moments in which your teen will match your past with your words.

Avoid:
> - Laughing about stories from your past.
> - Downplaying or evading the truth.
> - "Times were different back then."
> - Sounding out of touch with language related to this issue.

There are also some key validating phrases that can go a long way toward generally bridging the gap between you and your teen. (We'll get into specifics on the issues of drugs in later chapters.)

"Wow. I can see why this would be a confusing situation for you."
"Ouch. That must hurt."
"Would you like advice, or do you want me to just listen?"
"That must be so tempting."

What Not to Do

Parenting our kids through the teen years is certainly filled with challenges, and one of the big challenges is in figuring out the right relationship to have with them. We must avoid the three extremes: relating to our teens as though we're their contemporaries, relating to our teens as though they are adults, and relating to our teens as though they're children. We can't expect them to behave like adults, think like adults, or have adult maturity. On the other hand, we can't fall back on the simpler way of dealing with children when we sometimes resorted to *because I said so*. We can neither talk down to them as though they are not mature enough to think things through logically, nor talk to them like our peers, expecting them to figure everything out on their own.

Whatever you do, don't be unapproachable.

When asked what teens don't like about adults, the biggest complaint is that their parents don't really listen to them. Below I've listed some actual responses I received from teens when I asked them that very question:

> "They pretend to hear by grunting, nodding, even sort of laughing when they think they should, but offer no real response to show me they even heard what I said."

> "They don't ask any questions about what I said. They're too happy I stopped talking and are afraid to 'put another quarter in' [a phrase that parent actually uses]."

"Dad gets mad when I'm confused and just wants to spout out advice and expects me to take it without any further discussion."

"They're 'too busy.'"

"They say things like, 'Give me ten more minutes.' 'Not now, okay?' They aren't exactly rude, but they kind of brush me off."

"I know my mom loves me, but I just wish I could have a little face time for real."

Ouch.

You and I both know that pretty much whatever is bothering a teen will pass—maybe the next day or maybe next week. In a year, it will be a dim memory and other issues will have taken center stage. But more important than dealing with the specific issue or solving the immediate problem is to let your teen know that you take those problems seriously and care enough to listen to whatever they are. The feeling of rejection that comes when parents brush off concerns builds to an unidentifiable resentment that can lead to rebellion and anger. This is especially true when we're covering the issues that go along with addictions. If you are too busy to spend real time with your teens and to meet their emotional and spiritual needs, they're going to spend their time elsewhere, seeking to meet their needs in whatever way they can find.

Before you'll ever be able to make an impact regarding the hot-button issues in your teenagers' lives, you're going to need to gain their trust. They must believe that you're interested in whatever interests them, and should never feel that you're bored by their concerns. And much worse than thinking you're bored is believing that you're uninterested. Trust me, if your teens feel like you just want them to go away, they will.

> > > **Challenge:** *The next time your teen stomps into the house, grabs a Coke from the fridge, slams the door, and skulks toward the stairs, close your computer (no sighing allowed), smile, and ask her about her day. Then listen.*

Teenagers, like most people, have a tough time denying themselves pleasure in order to follow God or honor their parents. Our society assures us it's okay to do things just because we want to or because they're fun. Teenagers grow up with an if-it-feels-good-do-it mentality, and the minute they experiment and find out that alcohol and drugs can offer them a release or an escape from their struggles or some sort of reward like popularity, they've embarked on a pattern of behavior that will quickly lead to addiction.

As Christian parents, we believe wholeheartedly that God's Word hidden in the hearts of believers will guide them through life's tough choices and difficult moments. We know that's true, but until our kids live through pain and mistakes, until they've had a need to call on the Word of God themselves, it can be difficult to instill that dependency on God and His ways just because we say so.

So the big question, then, is:

> ➤ *How do we get our teens to care about God's Word?*

Whatever you do, don't preach.

No matter how much you study or how passionate you are about the nuggets of truth you uncover in the Word, if you don't pass along the truth in love, it's meaningless. Scripture should never be used to attack, browbeat, or belittle. It's also not meant to condemn. You should never, ever use Scripture to make your teens feel bad about themselves as people.

Preaching, lecturing, beating an issue into the ground . . . it falls on deaf ears. You most likely don't receive advice or instruction well if it's delivered in that manner, and neither will your teens.

Instead, speak the truth with love and respect.

Over the years, I've learned the hard way that knowledge spewed without love just sounds hollow. As a theology and doctrine junkie with a background in debate, I've turned far too many people away from the truth with unloving arguments and unrelenting attitudes. Here's what the Bible says about that:

> **If I speak in the tongues of men or of angels**, but do not have love, I am only a resounding gong or a clanging cymbal. If I have the gift of prophecy **and can fathom all mysteries** and all knowledge, and if I have a faith that can move mountains, **but do not have love, I am nothing**. (1 Cor. 13:1–2)

The message of Scripture will never reach our teens if they have knowledge of the *content* of the Bible without a grasp on the intent—the love. And without the proper *context*, its message and power will never reach our teens. The Bible cannot be applied simply as a rule book; it's far too easy to rebel against rules. It must be viewed as a love letter.

Teens can tell if you've really taken the Word of God to heart and applied it to your own life, or if you're just trying to do your spiritual duty by passing the doctrine on to them. They can tell if you're preaching out of control and fear, or if you're reaching out to them out of love and concern. You need to make clear that how you feel about certain behaviors is completely separate from how you feel about your teens as people.

Here are a few questions to ask yourself:
> - Have you prayed over the topic before bringing it up to your teen?
> - Are you taking biblical ideals and making them relevant issues for a teen?
> - Are you using too many personal examples or lectures?
> - Do your teens feel free to ask you tough questions? Are you prepared to give or find an answer if they do?
> - Are you offering application techniques, or just handing down rules?

Instead, model by making right choices.

Here's the tough part, Mom and Dad. Do you live in such a way that you are above reproach? I speak to myself on this point as well. How can we ask our teenagers, who are far less prepared to deal with life's temptations than we are, to make good decisions if we're not modeling those right choices and living a godly lifestyle in front of them? How can we expect them to overlook our shortcomings and choose better for themselves? When things get tough, you'd better believe they'll use our failures as an excuse to justify and excuse their own poor choices.

To help your teens reach toward the richest life possible, you need to be living as an example before them. In 1 Corinthians 9, Paul writes to the church about just this topic. He warns against preaching the truth to others but living in such a way that you miss it yourself.

> Therefore **I do not run like someone running aimlessly**; I do not fight like a boxer beating the air. No, I strike a blow to my body and make it my slave so that after I have preached to others, **I myself will not be disqualified** for the prize. (vv. 26–27)

Be honest about your struggles and temptations—let your teens know that it isn't simple for you either. Be open about the cost of doing the right thing so they'll know they aren't the only one dealing with temptation and sinful mistakes. Imagine if, when you were a teen, your parent had said to you, "You know what? I struggle with that too. It's not easy for me to make the righteous choice when it comes to _____ either. I do it because I know it's best for me and because I know God chose that as the way for me to walk, so I do my best to walk in it."

When teenagers can see their parents as human beings with weaknesses, failures, and struggles, they don't feel so alone in the battle. And when they see you clinging to God's promises for your life and theirs, they'll see the need for His Word in their lives.

Instead, provide "real-life" practice.

This is where the Hot Buttons series comes in. When we use the Strategic Scenarios game, purposeful dialogue about hot-button drug-related issues will provide us the opportunity to sneak in something resembling personal experience for our kids—without the dreaded ramifications—while also teaching them that their opinions, thoughts, and feelings are important and valid.

Here in part 1, I've discussed the whys, whens, and hows of confronting the tough issues in general, why to take a preemptive stand, and what to watch out for along the way. Part 2 covers the specifics of what your teens or preteens face these days in relation to substance abuse, addiction, and addictive behaviors. Some parents may feel that eight or nine years old is too young to talk openly about drugs, alcohol, and other addictive substances. These chapters will explain why I vehemently disagree.

In part 3, we'll actually do it. You'll be able to take away practical and precise words in the form of fifteen *Strategic Scenarios* for you to actually work through with your kids to press the hot buttons of addiction and substance abuse. Nothing helps a teen face tough issues like sustained, open communication with a godly, loving parent. I'll share truths about the topic, help you figure out how to handle it in your own home, and guide you in prayer as you ask God to help you with that particular issue.

CHECK POINTS ➤➤➤

CHECK POINTS

✓ Instead of trying to relate to your teen as a contemporary, instead of turning a blind eye during a toast at a wedding or allowing them a drag of Uncle Morey's cigarette, gain credibility with them by standing firm.

✓ They don't want you to fill the role of BFF; they want you to be the parent. Your kids get to choose from millions of potential friends in the world, but they only have access to a couple of parents.

✓ If you are too busy to spend real time with your teens and to meet their emotional and spiritual needs, they're going to spend their time elsewhere, seeking to meet their needs in whatever way they can find.

✓ Our knowledge of the content of the Bible, without giving it the proper context, will never reach our teens.

✓ You need to be clear that how you feel about certain behaviors is completely separate from how you feel about your teens as people.

✓ To help your teens reach toward the richest life possible, you need to be living as an example before them.

✓ When teenagers can see their parents as human beings with weaknesses, failures, and struggles, they don't feel so alone in the battle.

PART TWO

Identifying the Drug HOT BUTTONS

What do the hot buttons of addiction look like?

Are they the same for every person?

Will I know them when I see them?

Those are all questions we ask ourselves as parents all the time. It's important that we get answers to those questions for ourselves so we can move forward in preparing our teens for what lies ahead. It's natural for Christian parents to have an unspoken expectation that their kids are immune to some of the temptations and sinful choices made by other teens.

I catch myself assuming that my kids inherently get it on certain things, and then I wonder why I would dare assume such a thing. They aren't born with a perfect understanding of right and wrong and the resolve to always do the right thing; that has to be taught. Hopefully these next few chapters will enlighten you about the risks your teens face and help you prepare them for the tough choices ahead.

Substance
Addiction

What happened to that good little girl who used to climb onto my lap for a story each night? Where did that sweet little boy with the skinned up knees and grubby little fingers go? What about the ten-year-old who prayed for people and cried over the lost? When did that heart for Christ disappear?

Those are the questions Christian parents ask themselves—the things they beg God to answer—when their teens turn to drugs or alcohol. They remember happy, well-adjusted, energetic little kids with dreams and goals and big smiles across their faces. But now they see eyes shrouded in darkness, grim or vacant expressions, and sad or angry hearts.

Those parents are truly baffled. They never imagined that their children would face a battle with addiction. They're not sure how it started or when. The dreams that were birthed back when that precious little bundle was placed in their arms are shattered. Now they want someone to alleviate the guilt they feel each time they look at their child. Can there be healing? Are they to blame? Where did they go wrong? When will it end?

They are desperate for help.

What do you think they'd pay or sacrifice in order to go back to the moments before their addicted teen took that first sip or did their first drug?

Hopefully, you are not one of those parents. My prayer is that you've picked up this book in time to proactively prevent addiction from becoming a reality in your teen's life. I implore you not to think your family is somehow immune just because you go to church or do family devotions. Those are great things, but they're only the start.

If it's too late for you to deal with the issue of addiction proactively, don't lose heart. There is help for your son or daughter. And this book is just one of many resources available to help you through that difficult process.

How does an addiction start?

Every single addiction begins with a single grain of desire for something—anything. When germinated, that desire grows into a plant that must be continually fed. In a teen's life, that desire can be born from

- deprivation of relationship;
- desire for popularity; or
- desperation for escape.

When it blooms, the teenager feels fuller, richer, and rewarded. Then, when the blossom fades, the teen feels empty, lonely . . . longing to feel full again. That desire grows until it's uncontrollable and the teen is compelled to reach out and meet that need again. Thus begins the vicious circle, the cycle of addiction.

Parents, the truth is, most teens who drink, smoke, or use drugs do *not* become addicts. But genetics can play a part in predisposing a person toward addiction. A federal study funded by the National Institute on Alcohol Abuse and Alcoholism and published in *Pediatrics Magazine* concluded that 47 percent of alcoholics developed their addiction before age twenty-one, and 15 percent before age eighteen.[1] The problem is, you can't know the truth about the genetic makeup of your teenagers until it has already proven itself. You won't know if your teens are predisposed to alcoholism until they test it out. That's not a game worth playing.

Different brains deal with pleasure and need in different ways. So the point where use becomes an addiction is different for each person, and no one can truly know where his or her own tipping point is until it's too late. Teenagers have a harder time controlling their impulses to drink or use drugs than adults do because teens don't have as strong a grasp on consequences and lifelong effects, and their desire for experiences and testing boundaries often outweighs any perceived risk.

But a teen doesn't wake up one morning addicted to drugs or alcohol with no history of use. So let's take a look at the progression from start to addiction. There are five main stages on that often very short journey.

Stage 1 is simple *access* to drugs, alcohol, or other substances. Maybe Mom and Dad drink, maybe it's easy to acquire the substance locally, or maybe an older sibling is willing to provide. It's important to examine those factors and minimize the risks.

Substance Addiction

Stage 2 can range from *experimentation* or occasional use (monthly or even less) to *regular* weekly use of alcohol, tobacco, inhalants, or other drugs. At this stage, Mom and Dad are often unaware of what's going on. Don't be the clueless parent—open your eyes; you can still change the course of where this is headed by gathering information and acting swiftly and decisively.

In stage 3, the teen is well on her way toward dependence with *increased frequency* of use, even to the point of regular, daily use. Already, we may be looking at a teenager stealing to get drugs. If so, you must hurry; your son or daughter is slipping from your grasp into the clutches of addiction. You'll need to take whatever seemingly drastic measures are necessary, separating teens from friends and activities where there is opportunity for temptation.

In stage 4 of alcohol and drug use, we're well past experimentation and solidly on the way to addiction and a lifetime of hardship. At this point teens have become regular users, are *preoccupied* with getting high, and are experiencing academic and social problems as a result. You'll need help from a youth pastor, guidance counselor, or therapist who understands teens and addictive behaviors and their causes.

At stage 5, the young person only feels *normal* when they are using, high, or intoxicated—anything less feels uncomfortable and unnatural. During this stage, risk-taking behaviors like stealing, engaging in physical fights, or driving while intoxicated increase, and the teen becomes most vulnerable to having and/or acting on suicidal thoughts. They need help and so do you. This is beyond the scope of most parents' ability to handle on their own. The entire family needs to be involved, and outpatient or inpatient rehab is likely necessary.

Why didn't I notice?

When did it start, and why didn't I see the signs? Sometimes a life-changing event like a death or divorce can send a young person searching for escape. Other times it's some other sort of trauma like abuse, rape, bullying, a tough break up—or nothing tangible at all. It could be a subconscious need for attention or affirmation. If your teenager has a history of good behavior, it's tough to pinpoint the exact moment when things took a turn. What was the tipping point? Where did that one last temptation come from, and why did it have the effect it did when others in the past did not? Only you know the details about your family. I will say this, however:

> **If you're in this situation, now is not the time for guilt; it's the time for action.**

If you're not already dealing with a child in stages 3, 4, or 5, you can be proactive and watch for signs. It's impossible to give one description or list that will fit every situation. Just as every child is different, you'll need to be wise and creative in discovering what's going on in each one's life. You also need to be honest with yourself about the red flags that might pop up. Turning a blind eye will accomplish nothing.

Substance Addiction

Warning Signs

Some of the background or underlying issues that professionals believe contribute to addictive tendencies are:

- Need for immediate gratification
- Lack of consequences and accountability
- Overindulgence and entitlement
- Lack of or under-enforced rules and curfews
- Lack of responsibilities or low expectations placed on the individual
- Lack of physical or emotional safety (at home or elsewhere)
- Lack of quality time shared between parents and children
- Problems in the home like violence, addiction, or mental health issues
- Loneliness, hunger for relationships
- History of use and/or abuse in the family
- Easy availability of drugs, alcohol, and other substances
- Low self-esteem or a people-pleasing personality

Action Steps

Preventing is far better than curing. Addiction is definitely one issue that is much easier to tackle *before* it takes root. Once it's a problem in your teen's life, it's much more difficult to stop the progression and break the stronghold. Ensuring that drugs and alcohol are not accessible to your teens is the first step in prevention. That requires you to take the time and steps necessary to make sure that's the case wherever your kids go.

If you have alcohol in the home, put it under lock and key. Where else might your kids have access? Friends' houses. Parties. Youth group activities. Parental vigilance is the first step in prevention.

Lord, the issues of drug and alcohol abuse and addictions bring me to my knees. Please give me a holy peace about the risks and dangers associated with those destructive behaviors where my kids are concerned. Give me eyes to see what's really going on in their lives, ears to hear their needs, and the guts to take the steps necessary to really make a difference in my kids' lives. Grant me Your discerning wisdom so I can sort through the fears and the facts to always find the truth. Please protect my children from any kind of addiction, and even the temptation that could lead to experimentation. Amen.

CHECK POINTS ▶▶▶

CHECK POINTS

✓ Do not think your children are somehow immune to addiction just because you go to church or do family devotions.

✓ In a teen's life, addictive desire can be born from deprivation of relationship, desire for popularity, or desperation for escape.

✓ The point where use becomes an addiction is different for each person, and no one can truly know where his or her own tipping point is until it's too late.

✓ Teenagers have a harder time controlling their impulses to drink or use drugs than adults do because teens don't have as strong a grasp on consequences and lifelong effects, and their desire for experiences and testing boundaries often outweighs any perceived risk.

✓ Preventing is far better than curing. Addiction is definitely one issue that is much easier to tackle before it takes root.

✓ It's impossible to give one description or list that will fit every situation. Just as every child is different, you'll need to be wise and creative in discovering what's going on in each one's life.

✓ Ensuring that drugs and alcohol are not accessible to your teens is the first step in prevention.

Alcohol

Alcohol was very accessible to me when I was a teenager. I could easily get my hands on it in my home and had friends who could get hold of it outside my home. My dad drank quite a bit on a daily basis. He used to sit in his recliner when I was very little and yell "Pivo!" (Czechoslovakian for beer). My little brother and I would scamper to the refrigerator and scuffle over who could grab a can of beer first. We'd race back toward the family room and slide across the hallway tile to see who could return to Dad first with a cold one.

I wasn't allowed to drink as a teen—it was an understood no-no, but it wasn't something my parents and I talked about at any great length. Aside from the legal implications, it didn't really seem like my family was very opposed to it. And I drank anyway.

When all celebrations, happy times, holidays, special dinners, and events are marked with alcohol, we become conditioned to viewing alcohol in a positive light. Alcohol becomes a necessary ingredient in order to have a good time . . . or in order to get over a bad one.

Now, just for the record, I'm not here to talk about the rights and wrongs of alcohol use among adults. Arguments can be made for all sides of that debate, and all from a Christian perspective, but this Hot Buttons book is about our kids. Tweens and teens need to understand and buy into the fact that underage alcohol use is not only illegal but also dangerous to their present and future, and wrong according to Scripture if it leads to drunkenness or immoral behavior.

The only way to convey those truths so that your kids will take ownership of them and make a solid commitment to avoid alcohol in their own teen years and beyond is to have the conversations. It has to be an open and ongoing issue, brought up often, in a way that resonates with your teens.

How often do teens drink?

I'm sure it will come as no surprise when you hear that alcohol is the most common drug used by teens in the United States.

- Approximately three-fourths of adolescents have tried alcohol by the end of high school.[2]

- Approximately half of all teens drink alcohol on a monthly basis, and nearly half of those have been drunk at some point in the past year.[3]

- One-tenth of all teenage drinkers admit to binge drinking, which is usually characterized by consuming more than five drinks in a row.[4]

Those statistics are staggering. When I look at my own teens and their friends, I wonder which ones are drinking. I don't believe it could be one of my daughters, or my son—but am I alert enough to know for sure? Are you? Would you know the signs of intoxication? The smell of alcohol on the breath or skin, glazed or bloodshot eyes, personality changes, flushed skin, and disheveled appearance?

I'm a rather naive person, believe it or not. My husband can spot someone who's been using alcohol or smoking pot a mile away, but I never notice it. He thinks it's crazy that I can't identify the telltale signs in others. Because I don't naturally see it, I've had to train myself to open my eyes and look for signs in my kids. I don't want to turn a blind eye to destructive behaviors. I have a duty to my family and an obligation to God to be on guard.

Every teenager drinks, so what's the big deal?

Sadly, I'm well aware that many parents take the position that every teen is bound to experiment with alcohol and it's really no big deal. Some look the other way. Some allow drinking in their home. Some even provide alcohol to their teenagers themselves.

I'm trusting that's not you, or you probably wouldn't have picked up this book. However, let me take a moment to caution you against the mentality that opens you to permissiveness in this area. As teens get a bit older, many parents are so eager to be friends with their kids that they allow things they may never have thought they would. Moms or dads who share a drink or two with their teens brush it off, saying they'd rather have them do it at home than out at a party.

But do they really believe it stops at home? Or is it just a teaser for what's coming later at the party? These parents may be shocked by these statistics:

◀ In contrast to adults, teens tend to abuse alcohol simultaneously with other substances, usually marijuana.

◀ Male teens who drink heavily tend to complete fewer years of education compared to male teens who do not drink.

◀ Teens who drink are more likely to engage in sexual activity, have unprotected sex, have sex with a stranger, or be the victim or perpetrator of a sexual assault.[5]

Of course, whether teens or adults consume alcohol, there are many things that can go immediately wrong: lapses in judgment, drunk driving accidents, alcohol poisoning.

◀ More than three teenage drivers die in alcohol-related accidents every single day.[6]

But there are also long-term effects that can come specifically from underage drinking that won't necessarily occur when someone starts using alcohol later in life.

Alcohol inhibits a teen's ability to pay attention—and this isn't just at the time of the alcohol consumption. Poor attention span can follow a drinking episode and last for weeks. A recent study led by neuroscientist Susan Tapert of the University of California, San Diego compared the brain scans of teens who drink heavily with teens who don't. The team discovered damaged nerve tissue only in the teens who consumed alcohol. Those researchers believe this damage negatively affects attention span and the ability to comprehend and interpret visual information.[7]

In teens, vital areas of the brain are not finished developing, so they're more sensitive to the toxic effects of substances than an adult brain would be. The maturation of those key areas of the brain can be permanently impeded by alcohol.

Another very important fact for you to understand and convey to your teen is that the younger a person is when they begin drinking, the more likely they are to develop a problem with alcohol. In other words, partying as a teen makes a person more susceptible to alcoholism later in life. This is not something we should be willing to gamble with under the guise of being the cool parent. The cost is far too great for our kids and even for any potential grandkids. I don't know about you, but I don't want my grandchildren raised by an alcoholic, and I want no part in enabling that to happen.

Is my teen at risk for alcoholism?

Whether or not a teen is likely to take that first sip of alcohol and then follow the path to addiction can often be tied to the home life and to the relationship the teen has with his or her parents. Some of the family risk factors for teenagers to develop drinking problems include:

- Lack of (or minimal) parental supervision
- Lack of communication
- Excessive family conflicts

- Inconsistent or severe parental discipline
- Family history of alcohol or drug abuse

Often alcohol use is rooted in the home but, as with most things, there is no hard and fast rule. Sometimes a teenager simply makes a poor choice and gets trapped in a downward spiral. Certain personality traits or individual risk factors that make this a stronger possibility include:

- Impulsivity
- Tendency to follow the crowd—a people pleaser
- Emotional instability including depression or self-esteem problems
- Adrenaline junkie tendencies or thrill-seeking behavior
- Belief that alcohol use is not a risky behavior

Warning Signs

Most of the warning signs for alcohol use are the same as for any addiction: change in sleep patterns, secretiveness or evasiveness, mood swings, dropping grades, change in friends or hangouts, lack of interest in activities like sports, loss of interest in spiritual things, awaking fatigued instead of rested. Other practical clues would include popping lots of breath mints or gum, and being unable to explain where money was spent.

Perhaps you've seen those signs, and have narrowed in on the fact that your teen is using alcohol, and now you're wondering, *Is it too late?*

Medically, biologically, socially, and spiritually, there are many ways to help a teen addicted to alcohol. Relapse prevention helps identify triggers and deal with problem behaviors and patterns. Individual counseling helps to set measureable goals. Twelve-step programs like Alcoholics Anonymous utilize individualized drug-counseling methods as well as group therapy methods.

It's most important, though, to get serious about prayer and spiritual support. Doctors and scientists would tell you that belief in God as a higher power is fine, but it's really no different from ascribing spiritual status to a rock. I'm here to tell you that's a lie. That's exactly what your enemy, Satan, the father of lies, wants you to believe. If you turn your attention to a twelve-step program relying on anything other than Almighty God as your higher power, or if you help your teen put her faith into something like a stuffed bear, then Satan has succeeded in keeping the focus on a path of misplaced dependency and inadequacy.

Sure, people have been successful at breaking the chains of alcoholism without a faith in God, but why would you want to? Without the healing power of God and His strength and power, it's like swimming upstream. Why make it any more difficult than it has to be? He offers to carry the burden—let Him.

We serve a God who's in the business of healing. He longs to restore what your enemy has stolen and He will be faithful to complete the work He's begun in your teen. So, get the counseling, do the hard work, but follow through with the spiritual applications and put your ultimate dependency on Jesus Christ. Chapters 10, 12, 13, and 14 will guide you in doing that specifically.

Action Steps

So, you're wondering:

How can I prevent my teens from taking that first drink?
> ➤ You can't.

It's true. You really can't prevent it with 100 percent certainty. What you can do, though, is teach, train, guide, and model the behaviors you want to see mirrored back to you.

While your teen is in the first stage of addiction (having access to but not yet having used alcohol [see chapter 4]), you can take preventive measures by limiting or removing the access. Simple supervision is a vital deterrent to keep access from becoming use. If you're there, your teens can't engage in behaviors you don't allow. Teens are often left unsupervised between the time they get out of school and when their parents get home from work. Many teens drink then, out of mischief or boredom. Clubs, extracurricular activities, and sports are a healthy way to limit the time your teen spends alone in the house.

The stages of addiction can move slowly, or they can race by in a matter of days or weeks. It's far better to prepare and prevent than to react to an existing problem.

Some other ways to help prevent alcohol use among your teens:

> ➤ Communicate clearly and openly about the negative effects of alcohol as outlined in this chapter. Facts and figures usually don't have much of an impact to a teen, however, because consequences

beyond their next birthday are pretty much inconceivable. This is where you need to get creative, Mom and Dad. Figure out what motivates your teen and reach him there. Don't dump a bunch of facts all at once and expect them to sink in.

> Share in great detail what your expectations are in regard to alcohol—and why. Keep God's Word at the forefront of your discussion, along with your love for your teen and interest in her well-being.

> Be available for questions and dilemmas on this subject.

> Don't judge when the subject is broached—treat it as an opportunity.

> Work through Strategic Scenarios 3–6, 8, and 11–12, along with the study guides found later in this book.

Father, I lift up my teens to You right now. Please place a hedge of protection around them and help them stay focused on the prize. Help them withstand peer pressure and say no to alcohol use. Help me guide my teens to have a long-term perspective that understands goals and consequences rather than a short-term view that seeks worldly satisfaction. Show me what I need to see, and give me the right questions to ask so I can respond to situations immediately.

Thank You for loving them so much. Amen.

CHECK POINTS

CHECK POINTS

✓ Teens need to understand and buy into the fact that teenage alcohol use is not only illegal, it's dangerous to their present and the future, and wrong according to Scripture if it leads to drunkenness or immoral behavior.

✓ Teen alcohol use can drastically affect the development of the brain and dramatically increases the likelihood of adult alcohol problems.

✓ The younger a person is when they begin drinking, the more likely they are to develop a problem with alcohol.

✓ Simple supervision is a vital deterrent to keep access to alcohol from becoming use of alcohol. Limit or remove access wherever possible.

✓ The stages of addiction from access to abuse can move slowly, or they can race by in a matter of days or weeks. It's far better to prepare and prevent than to react to an existing problem.

✓ We serve a God who's in the business of healing. He longs to restore what your enemy has stolen and He will be faithful to complete the work He's begun in your teen. So, get the counseling, do the hard work, but follow through with the spiritual applications and put your ultimate dependency on Jesus Christ.

6 **Inhalants**

This may be the most important, eye-opening chapter in this book. Take notice of the facts . . .

A new generation of children is stepping into the dangerous world of inhalants. Data collected from the National Survey on Drug Use and Health show that 1.1 million twelve- to seventeen-year-olds acknowledged using inhalants in the year prior, and that almost 600,000 teenagers start using inhalants annually.[8] Shockingly, by eighth grade, one in five students will have gotten high from inhalants.[9]

When I was in high school, my friends and I sniffed correction fluid, permanent markers, and even gasoline to get high. We (or at least I) didn't do it often, but it was definitely a way to achieve a seemingly safe level of intoxication. It really did feel safe. I don't think a single one of us realized the effect it actually had or how dangerous it was. None of us would have said that we "did drugs"; even our parents probably wouldn't have been very concerned if they had known.

It's pretty common to think of drugs as the kinds of things you can only buy from a dealer in a back alley or on a street corner.

Most of us forget that substances at least as harmful can be found in our garage or under our bathroom sink. If a student carried around a baggie full of white powder, someone would ask questions. But what about Sharpies and Wite-Out? Those are simple school supplies. No one would ever raise an eyebrow at students carrying those, even though they emit dangerous and highly addictive chemical vapors that teens inhale on a daily basis, in every school. Also, there's no legal ramification to carrying around nail polish remover or a can of hair spray.

Legal?
> Yes.

Easily obtainable?
> Yes.

Safer than other drugs?
> Absolutely not.

One major problem is the fact that kids perceive the risk to be relatively low. In the upcoming sections, you'll see how that is a complete fallacy, but it doesn't change the fact that teens increasingly see inhalants as safer than street drugs. In a 2005 study, only 64 percent of teenagers acknowledged that inhalant use can cause death. And that number was *down* 19 percent from only four years prior. This is notable because rather than growing more educated about the risks, teens are becoming less aware.[10]

Another major problem is that other drugs—whether legal or illegal—are *meant* to be ingested. Inhalants were never meant to be ingested, and far from simply a *drug*, they are actually a *poison* to the human body.

What exactly are *inhalants*?

Inhalants come in at least four different forms and each has similar effects on the brain and the body.

Volatile solvents are fumes, actually liquids that become a gas at room temperature. They are not sprayed, they simply give off fumes that are inhaled. These include:

- paint thinners
- acetone
- nail polish removers and other paint removers
- gasoline
- certain glues
- marker fluids

The vapors can be sniffed, snorted, or directed right into the airways. They can also be sprayed into a plastic bag and inhaled right from there. Many people will spray a rag and then place it over the mouth and nose at the same time to increase the effects.

Gases include many household and commercial products:

- lighters
- propane
- whipped cream dispensers that contain nitrous oxide
- refrigerants

In case you're wondering, yes, the tip of a whipped cream dispenser can be pressed just enough to let the air escape without releasing the cream itself; the toxic vapors released are inhaled right from the tip of the dispenser. The latest trend is to siphon freon gas from an air-conditioning unit. Freon can freeze the lungs, cause frostbite of the airways, lead to cardiac arrest (heart attack), or cause brain damage.[11]

> "Even a single use can result in sudden death," says Dr. Shan Yin of the Cincinnati Children's Hospital. "Parents should be very concerned if they find out their child is using this."
>
> Gail Henry knows the heartbreak. Her 18-year-old son Jacob was found dead next to an air conditioning unit with a bag over his head. He had been huffing freon.
>
> "Don't ever considering doing it because that five seconds of high you get when you do it isn't worth dying over," she says.[12]

Nitrites are found in room deodorizers, air dusters, or sold in capsules, often called "poppers" or "snappers," which release inhalable vapors when opened or popped. Use of these substances relaxes the smooth muscles in the body and increases the heart rate.

Aerosol sprays. Consider these deadly inhalants easily found in your home:

- hair spray
- spray paint

◀ aerosol deodorant

◀ cooking spray

Teens and preteens spray the substance into a plastic bag and then inhale from the bag. It's as easy and cheap as that.

Unlike other drugs, the high received from inhaling a chemical substance only lasts a few seconds to a few minutes, but that's not a positive thing! Because it wears off so quickly, teens automatically reach for the next dose. This usually means the teenager is using over and over again throughout the day, unaware that even though the high may have dissipated, dangerous chemicals continue to build up in the body. Each exposure to the chemical opens them up to a debilitating or deadly reaction.

I'm going to state the obvious here: you can't possibly rid the world of all these things. You can't even render them completely inaccessible to your kids, so in relation to inhalants, *all* kids are already in stage 1 in the progression to addiction (see chapter 4). Education and openness are vital. You have to face this issue and talk about it openly and often.

What happens in the body during inhalant use?

When inhalants are used, the vapors enter the body and become absorbed by the brain and the central nervous system. That's enough to make me want to ensure that my kids run the other way. As with intoxication, bodily functions slow down. Symptoms like excitability, difficulty speaking or walking, agitation, and nervousness set in immediately.

Other short-term effects of inhaling chemicals include:

- Increased heart rate
- Hallucinations or delusions
- Loss of feeling or consciousness
- Nausea and vomiting
- Loss of coordination
- Slurred speech

Inhalants are incredibly addictive, both physically, including withdrawal effects, and psychologically. By the time they figure out their dependency, it's often too late for a teenager to quit; the harmful effects of inhalants can be irreversible. Because of the extreme addictive qualities of inhalants, and their accessibility, teens who use inhalants are likely to be long-term users and are at risk of:

- Brain damage
- Muscle weakness
- Depression
- Headaches and nosebleeds
- Permanent loss of sense of smell or hearing
- Bone marrow damage
- Immune system impairment
- Death

What are the risks?

Inhalants are as deadly—even more so, actually, than street drugs. This is so important to note because teens imagine the opposite is true.

Let's take a look at some facts:

> For every 1,000 exposures to inhalants, 5.5 people die. For comparison, that figure is only 0.4 deaths per 1,000 exposures to pharmaceuticals.

> Butane caused 58.1 deaths per 1,000 exposures (not per user)—almost 6 percent of the times butane is used to achieve a high, someone dies.

> Propane at almost 26 deaths per 1,000 exposures, air fresheners at almost 22, and nitrous oxide at almost 14.

> Paint and gasoline had the lowest fatality rates at 1.6 per 1,000 exposures.[13]

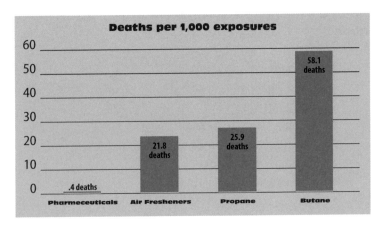

Deaths per 1,000 exposures

Notice, these figures are *per exposure*, not *per user*. Each user might be exposed several times a day.

Causes of death include:

Sudden sniffing death. This is the most common cause of death related to inhalant use. When the influx of vapors speeds the heart rate and slows other bodily functions, the heart goes into cardiac arrest—a heart attack. This happens at any age and is a direct result of inhalant use. It's just as likely to happen with the first use as it is to happen with the hundredth.

Asphyxia. Users start choking when toxic fumes squeeze the oxygen from the lungs.

Suffocation. This can occur when users inhale vapors from within plastic bags placed over the head, because the high brings about disorientation and diminished reflexes.

Common injuries. Users suffer from disorientation and lack of judgment, and put themselves in harm's way.

Suicide. Depression is a common side effect when the high wears off.

Inhalant use is not a game; it's not a benign way to achieve a little high. It's serious, extremely dangerous, and can easily slip under the radar until it's too late. You have to be intentional about watching for the signs of use because the products are readily accessible and simply unavoidable.

Warning Signs

If your teen is using inhalants, there will often (but not always) be noticeable signs. Watch for symptoms like mood swings, exhaustion, appetite changes, vomiting, dilated pupils, facial rashes or blisters, runny nose, coughing, and bad breath.

Action Steps

If you suspect your teen is using or has used inhalants, seek treatment right away. The resource section at the back of this book will help point you in the right direction. There's no time to waste; this is not a wait-and-see issue. Immediate action must be taken to uncover the truth, educate your teens (and their friends), and prevent any further use. Your child's life depends on it. I'm not an alarmist, but the facts don't lie. I won't sit back and let teenagers, uneducated about the issues, do stupid things that will cost them their lives. I hope you won't either.

> Be informed and available for questions on this topic.
> When the subject comes up, don't judge. Consider it an opportunity.
> Work through Strategic Scenarios 10 and 13.

Jesus, there's just so much out there that can entice my tweens and teens and lead them down a dangerous path—when I think about it all, I feel sort of helpless. Please guide me. Help me to steer them well and love them through it all. Give me the words to say and the wisdom to see the truth of what's going on. Remove my blinders. I also ask for Your protection to surround my kids as they face the temptations and trappings of this world and the attacks of their enemy. Give them a full measure of Your wisdom as they face and respond to peer pressure. Thank You for loving them so much. Amen.

CHECK POINTS

✓ In a 2005 study, only 64 percent of teenagers agreed strongly that inhalant use can cause death; and that number was *down* 19 percent from 2001. . . . Rather than growing more educated about the risks, teens are becoming less aware.

✓ Inhalants were never meant to be ingested, and far from simply a *drug*, they are actually a *poison* to the human body.

✓ Inhalants are serious, extremely dangerous drugs that slip under the radar until it's too late. You have to be intentional about watching for the signs of their use because the products are accessible to everyone.

✓ Because of the extreme addictive qualities and accessibility of inhalants, teens who use inhalants are likely to become long-term users.

✓ Since you can't make inhalants inaccessible to your teens, education and openness are vital. You have to face this issue and talk about it openly and often.

✓ If your teen is using inhalants, there will often (but not always) be noticeable signs. Watch for things like mood swings, exhaustion, appetite changes, vomiting, dilated pupils, facial rashes or blisters, nose running, coughing, and bad breath.

✓ If you suspect inhalant or other drug use, seek treatment right away. The resource section at the back of this book will help point you in the right direction.

OTC and
Prescription Drugs

The misuse of seemingly innocuous legal substances and medications prescribed by a doctor can pull a child into the world of substance abuse and cause a lifetime of battles. Kids who would never snort cocaine or mainline heroin will often pop a pill off the drugstore shelf because they believe it to be safe, legal, and just not that big of a deal. They can't really get in trouble for having cold medicine on them, right? And carrying around a prescription bottle of a medication that a doctor recommended isn't going to raise concern from most people. Whereas middle schoolers are more likely to use inhalants, older teens turn to these types of drug.

Prescription Medications

If we had to rank them, prescription meds would fall a step or two below illegal drugs, right? Well, though it may seem that way, let me assure you, they are equally dangerous and in many ways even more scary, because their use is easier to hide. If a kid is messing around with these for a few weeks and it goes unnoticed, it's fairly easy for her to try more or to move on to something else next.

Among youth ages twelve to seventeen, 7.7 percent reported the nonmedical use (misuse) of prescription medications in the last year. According to the 2011 Monitoring the Future survey, prescription and over-the-counter drugs are among the most commonly abused drugs by twelfth graders, after alcohol, marijuana, and tobacco. And prescription drugs are a gateway to further drug use; youth who abuse prescription medications are also more likely to report use of other drugs.[14]

How big of a problem could it really be?

> - Nationwide, 20 percent of teens say they've misused a prescription drug.[15]
> - Every day, on average, 2,500 teens use prescription drugs to get high for the first time.[16]
> - More than 70 percent of people who abuse prescription painkillers say they get them from a friend or relative; the vast majority are given to them by a friend or relative "for free" (55.9%), others are purchased from a friend or relative (8.9%), taken from friend or relative without asking (5.4%), or purchased from a drug dealer or stranger (4.3%).[17]
> - With the majority of teens (56%) agreeing the prescription medicines are easier to get than illegal drugs, teens see these substances as readily available highs.[18]

Opioids (such as the pain relievers OxyContin and Vicodin), central nervous system depressants (e.g., Xanax, Valium), and stimulants (e.g., Concerta, Adderall) are the most commonly abused prescription drugs.

Drugs such as OxyContin, Ritalin, and Vicodin have become so common among today's youth that more than 15 percent of high school seniors say they've taken at least one prescription or OTC pill for nonmedical purposes within the past 12 months. And in 2005, the National Survey on Drug Use and Health revealed that more than two million teens had abused prescription drugs that year alone.[19]

Teens can garner information about the effects of these drugs, either to be taken alone or mixed together, on the Internet. You might be surprised to find out that your teen knows Adderall and Ritalin will give them energy and a sense of euphoria while Vicodin will make them mellow. Teens know which drugs to use for which effect.

Over-the-Counter Medications

Over-the-counter (OTC) drugs are medications that can be purchased in a drugstore without a prescription. Cough medicines, along with medicines believed to help with weight loss—like laxatives, diuretics, and diet pills—are often abused. Many teens (and even adults) assume these drugs are less dangerous than those found only behind the pharmacy counter. After all, how could something so readily available be harmful? And, of course, taken as prescribed, there are little to no risks associated with these medications. But with misuse, all of these can have serious, potentially fatal, side effects.

One of the biggest problems with curbing teen OTC drug use is the fact that so few teens know about the dangers. Drug education programs focus mainly on illegal drugs and, likewise, parents tend to focus mainly on the dangers of illegal drugs like marijuana (which is also increasing in popularity among teens).

- 92 percent of parents claim to talk to their teens about drug use
- 60 percent of parents report speaking to their children "a lot" about marijuana use

BUT

- [only] 33 percent of parents report talking to their teenagers about the dangers of OTC medications to get high.[20]

Apparently, even parents underestimate the dangers of OTC medications, and fail to warn their children, even when they know that the medicine cabinet is readily accessible to everyone in the house and that medications not found there can be easily obtained with a few dollars and access to a drugstore.

Cold medicines

The most commonly abused OTC drugs include those that contain the ingredient DXM (dextromethorphan), a cough suppressant, which is found in medicines used to treat cold and flu symptoms and sinus pressure.

> More than half of teens (55%) don't agree strongly that using cough medicines to get high is risky.[21]

But these drugs can be used to cause a high just like illegal drugs and alcohol can. The big problem with the use of drugs containing DXM like Robitussin, antihistamines like Benadryl, or decongestants like Sudafed is that the typical early signs of drug abuse—excess spending, stealing to support the habit, drug paraphernalia, strange smells, hygiene problems— are typically not present with OTC abuse.

> One study reported that 6 percent of high school seniors reported use of cough or cold medicines to get high in the past year.[22]

It's easy for a teen to give it a try, and it seems safe compared to other dangers out there. Then the second time, it's even easier, until it's happening on a regular basis and parents have no idea it's going on.

> Carl Henon had just graduated from high school when one morning his mother, Misty Fetko, went to wake him.
> "Immediately, I knew something was wrong," she said. "I called 911 and I started CPR and I was just—I was basically screaming."
> Henon never woke up. He had overdosed on Robitussin cough syrup.[23]

Although his mom had warned him about illegal drugs, she had never considered the need to warn him against cough syrup, which Carl and his friends had been drinking regularly to get high.

Effects of DXM include:

- Agitation
- Dizziness
- High blood pressure
- Lack of coordination
- Distorted vision
- Vomiting
- Insomnia
- Paranoia
- Hallucinations
- Loss of muscle control
- Coma
- Death

Diet pills

Diet pills can create a mild buzz or energy rush. The effects a teen can gain from diet pills decreases with use, so more and more must be used to attain the same level of zing.

> Ephedrine, caffeine, and phenylpropanolamine are just some of the dangerous and addictive substances found in diet pills. Herbal, sometimes referred to as "natural," weight loss products can be just as dangerous as diet pills. All of these substances act as stimulants to the central nervous system and much like speed, can have serious and potentially fatal side effects.[24]

Teen diet pill abuse can also point to an eating disorder. I took weight-loss pills as a teenager; my friends passed them around like candy. It was considered to be a safe way to lose weight—a quick fix with an energy boost. Laxatives and diuretics may also be abused for the same purpose, and can cause dehydration and other health problems.

Other OTC medicines
- Caffeine stimulants like No-Doz
- Sleep aids like Unisom
- Motion sickness treatments like Dramamine
- Sexual performance drugs

Basically, anything that can be purchased legally that will alter the body or state of mind is dangerous. Some places are getting smart and restricting the purchase of OTC drugs by people seventeen and under, but this is far from a widespread control. Plus, the Internet makes the access to OTCs impossible to control. Anyone can order a two-pack of Nyquil from Amazon for under $15 with free, two-day shipping.

Warning Signs
Just like with all substance use, there are signs. Many of them are similar to the others we've talked about in this book already. The important thing, when we're talking about OTCs especially, is that you are intentional as you watch for danger since the obvious signs won't be evident until it's too late.

Watch for signs like:
- Your child taking a medication when not ill
- OTC drugs missing from the medicine cabinet
- OTC drugs or empty packaging in your child's room or backpack
- Falling grades
- Mood swings
- Changes in normal habits
- Changes in appearance
- Missing money
- Unexplained spending

Physical signs of OTC and prescription drug use include:
- Dilated pupils
- Sweating
- Dry mouth
- Red face
- High fever
- Slurred speech
- Blurred vision
- Nausea and vomiting
- Irregular heartbeat
- High blood pressure
- Numbness in fingers and toes
- Delusions
- Hallucinations
- Loss of consciousness

Be on the lookout for strange packages or unexplained purchases that are mailed to your home. Note empty medicine bottles in your trash, or if you find yourself replacing your cold medicine or other OTCs more frequently than you think is natural. Monitor your children's Internet search history for subjects dealing with OTCs and prescription meds.

Prevention, starting at an early age, is critical. You are your child's most important role model. Talk openly about the harmful effects of OTC and prescription drug abuse so your kids know that you're aware of this type of harmful activity. Help your teens find healthy ways to reduce stress.

Action Steps

◀ Since this is such a sneaky problem, it's vital that you talk about the issue with your kids Let them see your awareness and help them understand the dangers.

◀ Work through Strategic Scenarios 2 and 14.

Sometimes, when I think about the risks my kids face too much, I want to throw my hands up in the air and give up. I can't possibly keep them from making dumb choices and doing dangerous things. So I'm daily growing more and more grateful that I don't have to because You're on it. Thank You for guarding my kids and guiding me as I parent them. Help me to teach them and guide them into good choices and godly living, and please protect their bodies from the effects not only of drugs and alcohol but even legal substances. Please guard them and protect them from choices like drug use that can affect the rest of their lives. Thank You for holding this family in the palm of Your hand. Amen.

CHECK POINTS

✓ The perception of OTC drugs is that their legality somehow makes them safe. How could something so readily available be dangerous?

✓ Kids aren't informed of the dangers of OTC or prescription drugs. Drug education programs focus mainly on illegal drugs, and, likewise, parents tend to focus mainly on the dangers of illegal drugs like marijuana.

✓ It's easy for a teen to give it a try, and it seems safe compared to other dangers out there. Then the second time, it's even easier, until it's happening on a regular basis and you have no idea it's going on.

✓ More than 70 percent of people who abuse prescription painkillers say they get them from a friend or relative.

✓ Teens can garner information about the effects of OTC drugs, either to be taken alone or mixed together, on the Internet. . . . Monitor the Internet search history for subjects dealing with OTC and prescription meds.

✓ Prevention, starting at an early age, is critical. As with everything, you are your child's most important role model.

Illegal Drugs

All through my teen years and well past college, I was never even in the same room with illegal drugs—that I know of anyway. No one ever offered me any, and I never saw evidence of drug abuse in my friends. I'm sure it was there, the statistics from the era confirm it, but I was oblivious to it.

Now, a couple of decades later, drug use is just as prevalent, and I'm much more aware of it as I keep watch over my kids. My fourteen-year-old lives a relatively sheltered life in a small Midwestern town, but she's seen more drugs and has heard of more incidences of their use than I have in my entire life. I'm saddened by that, but I'm grateful my eyes are open to the realities so I can do the preemptive work necessary to attempt to spare her and my other children from a lifetime of addiction.

What causes teen drug use?

The risk factors for initial experimentation with drugs are much like the risks for alcohol abuse: minimal parental supervision, lack of communication at home, a high incidence of domestic conflict, abuse of any kind, and a family history of alcohol or drug abuse are the big ones; along with some of the individual traits like impulsivity, depression, and a predisposition to risky behavior.

Drug use is just like any sinful progression. It starts with the first flirt with experimentation and builds from there. The first time drugs are used is usually the toughest hurdle; after that, it gets easier because there is no longer fear of the unknown. Soon, the body starts to *crave* the high, and then shortly thereafter, it *needs* the high. Most, if not all, teen addicts will say they never wanted to do drugs, never thought they would, and, looking back, can't believe they wound up an addict. I have yet to find anyone addicted to drugs who didn't regret the path they took to get there.

What are the dangerous effects of drug use in teens?

Much like alcohol, the younger a person is when they begin using drugs, the more likely they are to develop a substance abuse problem, and the more likely they are to relapse when trying to quit. Tweens and teens are still developing, so drug use in those early years becomes part of a person's makeup. In effect, teens trade in part of their education, part of their lifelong success, and part of their personality for a quick high that will ultimately leave them feeling empty.

Drug use also removes inhibitions and makes teens more likely to have unprotected sex or sex with a stranger. It can cause mood swings and hallucinations and can mask but exacerbate other problems like depression and suicidal thoughts.

Another (very final) potential side effect of drug use is death.

A seldom-discussed aspect of teenage drug use involves the social and spiritual struggles inherent in a life controlled by the compulsion to alter consciousness. That's just a fancy way to say that when a teen wants to escape reality, relationships with people and with God will naturally suffer. The years that are supposed to be for growing, training, and learning become all about acquiring the next fix. The brain is so busy making it through its constantly altered state that it misses out on the education it should be receiving, and the social skills that normally develop during the teen years are nonexistent because drug addicts tend to pull away from healthy relationships.

What specific drugs should I watch for?

There are way too many drugs to name them all, but here are a few common ones you should know about:

Marijuana is a mind-altering drug that comes as a green, brown, or gray mixture of dried, shredded leaves, stems, seeds, and flowers of the hemp plant. It looks like dry herbs and is usually smoked as a nubby rolled cigarette or in a pipe or bong. Some users also mix marijuana into foods like brownies or use it to brew tea. It can be mixed with other drugs into deadly combinations. Marijuana is addictive, even though many try to say it isn't. About one in ten people who have tried marijuana at least once will become dependent on it.[25] In fact, there are more teens in treatment with a primary diagnosis of marijuana dependence than for all other illicit drugs combined.[26]

Cocaine, also known as *blow*, is an extremely addictive stimulant that directly affects the brain. Cocaine is usually a white powder that's sniffed or snorted, and in some forms it can also be shot into a vein. Risks of cocaine use include an increase in body temperature, heart rate, and blood pressure. Other commonly reported experiences are headache and abdominal pain often with nausea, decreased appetite, malnutrition, irritability, excitability, restlessness, anxiety, and paranoia.

Club drugs like Ecstasy, GHB, and Rohypnol (a date rape drug) are very popular and seen as fun drugs. They can be anything but fun, as they often lead to sexual indiscretion and even rape, not to mention overdose and death.

LSD or *acid* comes in tablets, capsules, or liquid. It is odorless, colorless, and has a slightly bitter taste. Often LSD is added to absorbent paper, such as blotter paper, and divided into small squares, with each square representing one dose. Those papers are placed on the tongue for rapid absorption into the bloodstream. It's commonly accepted that acid is not physically addictive, but it is habit-forming when users become mentally addicted to the effects.

Illegal stimulants like *Methamphetamine*, or *Speed*, are highly addictive drugs that affect the central nervous system. The immediate effects are described as euphoric, but that feeling quickly wears off, leaving the user desperate for more. The use of stimulants like caffeine pills, energy drinks, and diet drugs can be a gateway to the use of amphetamines (see chapter 7).

Warning Signs

Even more than knowing the individual drugs, it's important to know what signs to watch for in your teenagers. They can be sudden, glaring changes that scream for your help, or they can be subtle trends that creep in slowly like a sinister fog. If you're not observant, the fog will overtake your teen.

The symptoms fall into three categories: emotional, behavioral, and spiritual.

Specific emotional changes that can signal drug use include:
  - ➤ Irritability
  - ➤ Aggressiveness
  - ➤ Mood or attitude changes
  - ➤ Depression
  - ➤ Excitability
  - ➤ Restlessness
  - ➤ Drastic mood swings

Behavioral changes might include:
  - ➤ Lack of care for personal hygiene
  - ➤ Major shift in personal style, such as clothing and hair
  - ➤ Weight loss or gain
  - ➤ Drowsiness or sluggishness
  - ➤ Bloodshot, watery, or glazed eyes
  - ➤ Clumsiness
  - ➤ Drop in grades
  - ➤ Lack of focus

Illegal Drugs

- ➤ New group of friends; cutting ties with old friends
- ➤ Lying or making excuses
- ➤ Stealing
- ➤ Breaking curfew
- ➤ Withdrawal from the family or activities
- ➤ Verbal or physical abuse toward others

And spiritual alarm bells might include:
- ➤ Pulling away from church or youth group
- ➤ Avoiding prayer or other spiritual connections
- ➤ Expressing doubt or disbelief

Of course, if you find paraphernalia connected to drug use, that is cause for immediate concern: rolling papers, pipes, matches, pill bottles, mirrors, needles, syringes, tourniquets. You should also watch for blatant signs of intoxication or crash. Since the symptoms are so diverse depending on the actual substance being used and on how far the dependence has gone, you should be willing to seek medical and spiritual help if you have any suspicions of drug use.

Action Steps

- ➤ Closely monitor your child's activities and friends. (See *Hot Buttons Internet Edition* for advice on setting guidelines for and monitoring Internet activity. And *Hot Buttons Dating Edition* will help with all things dating related.)

- Work through Strategic Scenarios 1, 2, 7, 9, 14, and 15 in chapter 11.
- If you have any suspicion regarding drug use and your teen, act on it at once. Ask questions. Look through possessions. Have your teen tested for drugs if necessary
- If you have evidence that your teen has used drugs, get help, for yourself and for him or her. Immediately.

Don't keep drug use a secret. It may be embarrassing that *your* kids used drugs, but by telling others, you may help other parents to be aware and watchful for their own kids' activities. But also, you'll widen the watchful eye over your own child. Tell school authorities, church leaders, coaches, anyone who has access to teens and influence in your child's life. They will help you be vigilant, as you seek to help your child make right choices. Parents guide and direct, but ultimately, kids make their own choices. While it may seem embarrassing at first, in the long run, your loving intervention has a greater likelihood of making a difference in your teen's life than your fearful secrecy.

It's so scary, Lord. I love my kids so much, and I just want to shield them from all the craziness out there, but I just can't be everywhere at all times. Help me let go of them enough that they can grow in You, but shelter them enough to protect them from their enemy. Please guard them and protect them from choices like drug use that can affect the rest of their lives. Please help me to see what I need to see and then respond in effective ways. I need You with me, guiding me as a parent. Thank You for Your presence and Your protection. Amen.

CHECK POINTS

✓ The younger a person is when they begin using drugs, the more likely they are to develop a substance abuse problem and the more likely they are to relapse when trying to quit.

✓ The first time drugs are used is a hurdle; after that, it gets easier because there is no longer fear of the unknown. Soon the body starts to crave the high, and then shortly thereafter, it needs the high.

✓ In effect, teens trade in part of their education, part of their lifelong success, and part of their personality for a quick high that will ultimately leave them feeling empty.

✓ More teens are in treatment with a primary diagnosis of marijuana dependence than for all other illicit drugs combined.

✓ Drug use removes inhibitions and makes teens more likely to have unprotected sex or sex with a stranger.

✓ Since the symptoms are so diverse depending on the actual substance being used and on how far the dependence has gone, you should be willing to seek medical and spiritual help if you have any suspicions of drug use.

✓ While it may seem embarrassing at first, in the long run, your loving intervention has a greater likelihood of making a difference in your teen's life than your fearful secrecy.

PART THREE

Pressing the Drug HOT BUTTONS

We've discussed the dangers of drug and alcohol use and the trappings of addiction. We've looked at Scripture. We've addressed the probabilities of what your teens will face in the coming days, or what they've already been exposed to. Now it's your turn. It's time to do the work. It's time to take a stand in your home and claim your teens' hearts and minds for the Lord.

It takes work to reach the hearts of teenagers to help them become conscientious servants of God who take ownership of their own choices, and responsibility for their own well-being. It takes hard work to lead your teen to choose God's ways over the world's ways and to deny themselves the immediate gratification that comes with sin and wrong or premature choices.

Are you ready?

Protective Procedures

The best protection against drug use is avoidance. If you can help your kids avoid that first taste of alcohol or first dabble with drugs, you've won the battle. As I've said, the first use of any drug is the biggest barrier to the landslide that leads to regular use and addiction. Beyond that first move, it gets easier and easier to give in to peer pressure and to turn to drugs and other harmful substances. Earlier in this book we looked at the five main factors that put kids at risk for alcohol and other drug abuse—minimal parental supervision, lack of communication, excessive family conflict, inconsistent discipline, and family history of drug use. While I don't tackle these five areas specifically in the paragraphs that follow, you'll find them cropping up repeatedly as we seek to create homes where kids are safe, loved, nurtured, and raised in the Word.

Examine yourself first.

Regarding alcohol and other drugs . . .

Are your teens confused by the disparity between what you say and what you do? Do you communicate how you feel about all aspects of alcohol and drug use? If your teen compared your habits or practices with what you say and what you portray at church or anywhere else, would he find you hypocritical? If you smoke, for instance, how do you convince your teens not to participate in activities that are potentially harmful or fatal to their bodies? It's important to your teens' choices regarding this issue that you live an open, honest, and transparent life.

Supposing that you do, in fact, drink some alcohol, how do you balance that with your responsibility as a parent of tweens and teens? Here are some questions you should ask yourself:

- Am I using alcohol to escape reality or take the edge off a hard day?
- In social settings, do I drink in order to fit in or have fun?
- Is there a certain time of day when, or certain place where, having a drink always comes to mind?
- Can I stop at one drink? Do I drink without getting tipsy?
- Could I take it or leave it? Or am I so attached to alcohol in my life that I'd miss it if I couldn't have it?

"I have the right to do anything," you say—**but not everything is beneficial.** (1 Cor. 6:12)

Regarding your priorities . . .

Are you home when your kids are home? Are you too busy to monitor their activities and to know who their friends are? Have you supplied wholesome activities to fill in the gaps when you are unavailable? Are boundaries, curfews, and discipline inconsistent because you are not around to enforce them? Mom and Dad, if you said no to any of these questions, you need to reprioritize. Make sure that your kids realize that their well-being is one of your top priorities.

Regarding your relationships . . .

Are you able to settle conflicts without resorting to shouting or physical violence? Do you approach conflict in order to resolve it, or do you back into a corner until it evaporates? Your kids are learning their coping mechanisms from you, Mom and Dad, and you need to be sure that your kids don't view drug use as an acceptable or preferable alternative to healthy communication. You don't want to create an environment that they are motivated to seek escape from.

Interact with your kids frequently.

Have a conversation with your children—don't talk at them. Explore their thoughts; learn from them how they feel about substance use. Let them share fears, desires, temptations, and real stories about what they're seeing at school. Listen attentively, without judgment, and ask questions.

Everyone needs to know they are wanted and loved. Parents can either pour into that need and lay a strong foundation in their kids' lives, or they can work against it. There's no middle ground. Let your kids know you are interested in what they think and how they feel about any topic, whether it's drugs, alcohol, inhalants, or any other issue that can lead to worldly entrapment or sin. When your children share their feelings with you, praise them for being open. Create an expectation of reward for openness. Correct misinformation gently, and reinforce your values whenever possible.

Give them your most precious commodity: time. Be available and approachable at any time, for any reason. It doesn't matter if you get awakened three hours after you've fallen asleep and it concerns something you don't see as an emergency—treat it as the most important thing on the planet. How you handle those situations will determine whether your kids come to you with the big stuff and trust that you'll respond as a parent to their immediate needs, fears, and concerns. Once you have that kind of connection, you'll be able to share information and respond to questions in ways that will resonate with the belief system they are developing for themselves.

Make your home a place your teens and their friends want to hang out. That way you'll see more of them, know their friends, and hear what topics are on their minds. You can best protect them from poor, impulsive decisions in your own home.

Talk specifically about drugs.

The communication you have about substance abuse and addiction cannot be a onetime deal. It should be an ongoing, intentional part of the relationship you have with your kids. The conversation you should be having with your teens about addictions is an ongoing one that's as much a part of your family's practices as having dinner. Start the conversations when your kids are young, and make it clear that you are always willing to talk about these issues—whenever questions come up for them, or when a teachable moment occurs.

Teach them how to say no.

The saying is "Just say no." That's often easier said than done, isn't it? The word no, itself, doesn't hold the power; it's the heart and soul behind the word that makes the impact. Teach your children from a very young age how to say no like they mean it. It's not a question. They should make no apology or even try to convince others that they're right. They don't have to give a reason or make any excuses. No means no, and that's enough. If the pressure continues, they should walk away and send the message that the no is nonnegotiable and approval is not needed.

Be on the lookout.

Be watchful, Mom, Dad, Guardian. Look back in previous chapters at the lists of emotional, behavioral, and physical changes that may occur when kids are using drugs. Just because you see some of these things in your teen doesn't mean that there's definitely something dangerous going on, of course. Some of those changes will naturally occur with puberty. Several of them coming on all at once, however, could be a signal to a bigger problem. These symptoms should encourage you to dig a little deeper and watch a little closer. No symptom you observe will ever come close to matching the power of your gut feeling. If you're in prayer and asking the Lord to reveal any troublesome spots in your teens' lives, then that gut feeling is most likely the Holy Spirit answering your prayer.

Set loving boundaries.

It's vital that you're a nonjudgmental listening ear. That doesn't mean that you don't call out what's right and wrong and what you know is best for your teen. It's not what you say; it's how you say it. Your teen should feel that, no matter how wrong he or she has been, you are a source of love and acceptance.

This is a good time to instill a rule (or better yet, a promise) that you're never more than a phone call away.

Make sure your teens know they can call you at any time and you will show up, no questions asked, to remove them from any situation.

Now, the no-questions-asked part doesn't mean forever—it isn't a get-out-of-jail-free card. It simply means that you aren't going to browbeat them in the heat of the moment. You'll extricate them from the troublesome position they're in—no matter how they got there, even if it means they lied or disobeyed—and you'll deal with the details later, perhaps the next morning.

Further recommendations:

- Begin talking openly about this subject now. Don't wait until you fear they've already been experimenting with alcohol or drugs.
- Work through the fifteen Strategic Scenarios in chapter 11 and use them to teach your tweens and teens about choices, personal responsibility, and consequences.
- Invite your teen to open up to you by asking safe questions like: *What do you see going on at your school in relation to alcohol and drugs?*

> *How do your friends feel about alcohol and drugs?*
> *Do they feel pressured?*
> *Do they pressure you?*

- Establish a curfew if you haven't already.
- Give your teen sensible guidelines for being in a vehicle with other teens. (Check your local laws on this too.)
- Discuss drinking alcohol or using drugs and driving—rules, consequences, dangers.
- Identify the consequences for lying to parents about *who, what, when, where,* or *why.*
- Discuss the rules and consequences about having friends over while parents are absent, or of being somewhere else without parental supervision.

While the world laughs as we continue to abide by biblical standards, Christian parents must be prepared to stand in the gap for their children, even in terms of substance use and abuse. Sometimes we will need to make unpopular decisions, but they will always pay off in the long run. Parents, we need to be available to our children. We must have our proverbial doors open at all times so our children are comfortable coming to us with questions about sin and choices. Teens should not have to answer those questions alone. Allowing them to decide for themselves (or worse, allowing them to make their decisions based on what they see on television or in school) is setting them up for failure.

As parents, we must constantly recall Ephesians 6:4 (NASB):

> Fathers, **do not provoke your children to anger**, but
> bring them up in the discipline and instruction of the Lord.

If we live out this verse, our children will have the values of Christ instilled within them, and we can prayerfully trust that they will one day be ready to stand as adults and thrive as Christians amid the challenges of life.

The Armor
of God

As it pertains to the hot-button issues of drugs and the strongholds they can have over your teens, the "armor of God" is not simply a word picture in Scripture but a practical resource for navigating the spiritual battles Christ-followers face. Before you move forward to attack these addiction hot buttons in the next few chapters, I want to lead you through a symbolic application of the armor of God.

Below, you'll find a breakdown of Ephesians 6:10–17. Each phrase is followed by a bit of commentary and application, and a few directions. But please take note, there is nothing divinely pre-scribed in these specific directions. Perhaps there are other actions you can take that will hold greater meaning for you; in that case, feel free to improvise. However, please take this seriously. More than a silly exercise, this is a physical display of your faith in God's power and your acceptance of His protections.

> Finally, **be strong in the Lord** and in his mighty power. (Eph. 6:10)

Mom and Dad, you're not alone. All of the strength and wisdom you need to be a godly parent is already yours through the power of the Lord. You don't have to have all of the answers about drugs—He does. You don't have to see the future—He does. You don't have to make up for the past—He did. You don't have to have eyes in the back of your head or some kind of supernatural vision into your children's lives—because He does.

Do this: Raise your open hands in surrender, ready to receive from God and expectant that He'll grant you strength, wisdom, and grace.

Pray this: *Lord, please help me stand strong in the power of Your might. Help me to let go of my need to control, and help me to surrender my family to You. Let me rest in Your power and walk as a parent in Your strength. Guide my senses with Your knowledge and help me to know what I need to, when I need to, especially as it pertains to the issues of drugs and alcohol in my teenagers' lives.*

Put on the full armor of God, so that you can take your stand against the devil's schemes. (Eph. 6:11)

God has already provided your protection and has already secured your ultimate victory in the parenting battle—even if the battle seems daunting at time. Remember the promise in Philippians 1:6, where it says that He started the work (in your teens), and He'll finish it. He stands ready to uphold you as you face the enemy that seeks to pull your teens down a slippery slope.

Do this: Gird your shoulders; plant your feet. Stand proud like a soldier waiting for orders.

Pray this: *Prepare my body to receive Your armor. Place it carefully that I might be protected as a parent from doubt, fear, and other attacks of the enemy. Then, protect my kids in the same way, Father—their eyes, hands, mouths, and bodies . . . and guard their desires and decisions. Let them run from danger and stand strong against temptation when it comes to addictive behaviors and other sin.*

For **our struggle is not against flesh and blood**, but against the rulers, against the authorities, against the powers of this dark world and **against the spiritual forces of evil** in the heavenly realms. (Eph. 6:12)

You see, your real fight isn't against the friends, the peer pressure, the drinkers and partyers. It isn't against the desires that lurk inside every human being. And it isn't against your teen. It's against the enemy who seeks to destroy.

Do this: Place your hands on your teen's bedroom door.

Pray this: *Father, I surrender this child, whom You love with a passion far greater than even mine, to You. I call on Your mighty power to fight against our enemy who has no place in this family. We choose this day whom we will serve; we choose to serve You. And I claim Your promises*

The Armor of God

over the inhabitants of this home. I pray that no stronghold will take captive any of the children in this home.

Therefore put on **the full armor of God**, so that **when the day of evil comes**, you may be able to **stand your ground**, and after you have done everything, to stand. (Eph. 6:13)

Armor is the barricade between the enemy's attempts to cripple the followers of God and your heart, mind, and body. With the armor of God in place, Satan is ultimately powerless against you. We've read the end of the Book, and we know how the story ends: in the end, we win! But though the ultimate victory is assured, we may feel like we lose some of the battles along the way. We might get discouraged at times. That's when we need to rest in God's power, rely on His promises, and stand firm without fear.

Do this: Close your eyes and imagine impenetrable steel covering every inch of your body and your teen's body.

Pray this: *With armor in place, I stand proud as a soldier fighting for my family. I visualize the armor covering my child's head, heart, and soul. I stand confident in Your promises.*

Stand firm then, with **the belt of truth** buckled around your waist . . . (Eph. 6:14a)

The belt is a foundational and essential part of a warrior's armor because it actually holds the weapons. Without the belt, the solider would enter the battle unarmed. As parents, we need to prepare our kids for spiritual battle by arming them with the truth—the Sword of the Spirit—that is carried in the belt.

Do this: Buckle a proverbial belt around your waist. Then do the same in front of you as though your teens are present.

Pray this: *With Your truth around our waists, let it restrain our fleshly desires and poor choices and lead us on Your path.*

. . . with the **breastplate of righteousness** in place . . . (Eph. 6:14b)

The breastplate protects the heart.

Do this: Move your hands in front of your body and in front of you, representing your kids.

Pray this: *Let Your righteousness, oh Lord, be a shield about this family. You are our protector and the lifter of our heads.*

. . . and with your feet **fitted with the readiness** that comes from **the gospel of peace**. (Eph. 6:15)

The Armor of God

You're ready. You have the information you need and you're covered in prayer. In the next chapters, you're going to actually implement the principles of getting and staying battle ready.

Do this: Lift each foot and plant it down hard.

Pray this: *I am confident in Your Word, Lord. I believe that You have led me and prepared me to be my teens' very best advocate in this world. I am prepared to fight as Your ambassador, ready with Your Word.*

In addition to all this, take up **the shield of faith**, with which you can extinguish all the flaming arrows of the evil one. (Eph. 6:16)

Notice the shield is active, not simply defensive. You're not blocking the enemy's arrows and sending them back out to do damage somewhere else, you're extinguishing them. Apply that to the evil that lurks in the world of drugs, alcohol, and addictions.

Do this: Raise your arm as though you hold a shield and wave it in front of you. Imagine your kids standing before you, and wave it in front of each of them also.

Pray this: *Put out the flames, Lord. Let this shield of my faith swallow them whole that they would disappear.*

Take the **helmet of salvation** . . . (Eph. 6:17a)

The helmet protects your mind from doubt, fear, anger, carelessness, and apathy.

Do this: Place the helmet of salvation securely over your head, to your shoulders. Reach out in front of you and do the same as though your teens stood before you.

Pray this: *I rest in my salvation, Lord. You are mighty to save and faithful to preserve.*

. . . and **the sword of the Spirit**, which is the word of God. (Eph. 6:17b)

You're armed and ready to fight. In the following chapters, I will walk you through the next action steps in your battle for your tweens and teens.

Do this: Raise your sword, which is the Bible—the Word of God.

Pray this: *I am equipped and ready to fight Satan's schemes against my kids. I need You to guide me and show me what my next move should be. Keep my heart and mind open to the truths and possibilities of what my kids face. And help them, Lord, to have the strength to say no, the wisdom to walk away, and the passion to chase hard after You. Amen.*

The Armor of God

Strategic Scenarios   **11**

The first few chapters of this book identified why it's necessary to proactively press the hot buttons with your tweens and teens—and gave a few guidelines for when and how to do that. Part 2 outlined the specific hot buttons associated with the addiction, inhalants, and various drugs, both legal and illegal. You have prayerfully put on the armor of God. Now it's time to affect real change and make a lasting impact in your home by using Strategic Scenarios.

You'll begin by telling your tween(s) and/or teen(s) a short story as though it's actually happening to them. You'll then present them with a few optional responses to the situation, without giving them any indication of which response you think is better or worse, and allow them to choose the most natural personal response. Once they make their choice, you will lead them through the discussion points and refer them back to relevant material you learned earlier in this book. At the end of each discussion, you should give them the opportunity to change their original decision if they desire, and invite them to commit to wise choices in the future.

The important thing, when you begin this process, is to pray for guidance. You want to be open to the leading of the Holy Spirit so you can discern when to push an issue, and when to let it be. Don't bombard your kids with topics all at once. Take it slowly and alternate between the various issues presented in the Hot Buttons book.

You don't have to pretend you're making all this up as some big stroke of genius. It's okay to admit you're reading a book and this practice was suggested. After all, why not show your kids that you vigorously pursue new ways to reach and teach them? Trust me, once you begin, even if you're simply reading from the book at first, the conversation will develop; kids are desperate to work this stuff out.

In my family, these worked best around the dinner table. Sometimes we'd get through two or three over the course of a meal, but often just one would spark enough discussion and we wouldn't get any further. That's okay—in fact, that's wonderful. Communication is the goal, so don't stifle that in order to move on to the next scenario.

Some other places you might open Strategic Scenarios discussions are:

- in the car
- in a waiting room
- on a walk or bike ride
- while on a family date night

So, pretty much anywhere a conversation can take place!

If you have children of varying ages, don't shy away from doing these together. I'm a firm believer in getting the issues out on the table well in advance of the peer pressure. So, if your slightly younger children are going to be introduced to a concept relatively soon anyway, you'd much rather it come a bit sooner through these controlled and monitored means. And if the gender of the character in the scenario doesn't work in your family, make the necessary adjustments. But if you have kids of both genders, it's good for them to consider scenarios from the opposite point of view.

As you approach each topic, be careful not to preach. Allow your kids the freedom to work out the issue in this safe environment. Enjoy this process as it opens the lines of communication between you and your kids.

I won't lie, Mom and Dad, this is going to take work—lots of work. Are you ready for that? Are you convinced that you must put the time in with your teens and wage the battles now to help them win the war? Drug use and addition are very real and lasting concerns in our society and for our teenagers. The problem isn't going away, and it can't be ignored. It's also not an issue your kids can figure out alone. Don't leave this one to chance, parents. Put in the time with Strategic Scenarios and reap the rewards.

Parents, tell your teen this story.

Your very best friend who is also a Christian has been smoking pot on a regular basis. You've tried to confront the issue privately, but it hasn't stopped. You're starting to get worried that your friend might be addicted. What do you do?

Now offer the following options with no personal commentary.

Let your teen think about the choices and make an honest decision.

A. It's really none of your business. You can try to talk sense into your friend, but ultimately, it's not your decision, so you leave it alone.

B. You tell your friend that the pot smoking must stop or you'll have to tell your parents about it.

C. You're curious about marijuana so you ask to try some.

D. You bring the issue right to your parents and let them handle it.

Crucial Step

Use this scenario as a jumping-off point for a discussion about drug use. Be very careful not to sound judgmental or accusatory. Remember, your teen is exploring thoughts and first impressions—these aren't actual choices . . . yet. Parents, keep your cool no matter how your kids respond; you want to make open discussion a natural part of your relationship with them, not a minefield they need to navigate.

Discussion Points

- Why did you make the choice you did?
- Marijuana is dangerous. Contrary to what people say, it *is* addicting.
- Driving while high is deadly.
- Consequences to drug use can be life-altering. There are legal, social, physical, and educational implications.
- How do you feel about drugs in general? Is pot considered a lesser drug among your friends?
- Do you now have a different view on this scenario than you did at the start? Why or why not?
- Would you like to change your answer or stick with it?

To one who knows the **right thing** to do and **does not do it**, to him **it is sin**. (James 4:17 NASB)

Parents, tell your teen this story.

You're so busy! Between sports, homework, youth group, and spending time with friends, you're hardly sleeping. It's really taking its toll on you and you've been falling asleep in class. Recently you even got into some trouble for dozing off and not paying attention, and you risk losing your spot on the team. Your friend is concerned about you and offered you a little pill to help you stay awake. If it works, you can buy more. It could be the answer to your problem. What do you do?

Now offer the following options with no personal commentary.

Let your teen think about the choices and make an honest decision.

A. You have to try something or everything is going to start crumbling around you. You take the pill. If it works, you'll ask for more.

B. You try it one time—but only once. You just need to get more sleep.

C. You turn down the drugs and let a parent know about the offer.

D. You decline the offer and organize your schedule a little better so you can get more rest.

Crucial Step

Use this scenario to guide a discussion about speed and other energy supplements. Be very careful not to sound judgmental or accusatory. Remember, your teen is exploring thoughts and first impressions—these aren't actual choices . . . yet. And this is a great time to set some guidelines for the use of legal stimulants. Are you okay with coffee and caffeinated drinks? When and how much? What about energy drinks?

Discussion Points

- Why did you make the choice you did?
- What kind of friend would offer you drugs as a solution to your problem?
- The effects of speed go far beyond just staying awake. See chapter 8.
- Even possession of speed is against the law.
- What are some healthy alternatives to amphetamines?
- How do you feel about your current schedule?
- How often do you feel sleepy in class or while driving?
- Do you now have a different view on this scenario than you did at the start? Why or why not?
- Would you like to change your answer or stick with it?

It is useless for you to work so hard from early morning until late at night, anxiously working for food to eat; for **God gives rest to his loved ones**. (Psalm 127:2 NLT)

Strategic Scenario 3

Parents, tell your teen this story.

You're at a family wedding and everyone's having a great time. Many of your cousins and other teenagers are having a drink or two. No one seems to mind, and many of the adults seem to think it's kind of funny. You approach the bar to order a Coke and your favorite uncle offers you an alcoholic drink of some kind. You're intrigued, and it is a family member after all. What do you do?

Now offer the following options with no personal commentary.

Let your teen think about the choices and make an honest decision.

A. Why not go for it? Your parents can't get mad since it was your uncle who offered it to you. You've always wondered what the fuss is; now's your chance to find out.

B. You take a quick sip just to taste it, then hand it back and ask for a Coke. You don't want your parents to see you with an alcoholic drink in your hand.

C. You laugh it off but decline. You don't want to get in trouble.

D. You decline, and then go tell your parents. You want to make sure they see your commitment to not drinking, but you also want to make sure your uncle doesn't offer alcohol to any other teens.

Crucial Step

Use this scenario to guide a discussion about adults offering alcoholic beverages to minors. Be very careful not to sound judgmental or accusatory. Remember, your teen is exploring thoughts and first impressions—these aren't actual choices . . . yet. It can be confusing for teens to figure out when it's okay to trust other adults, and when they shouldn't. Prepare for open discussion on that issue.

Discussion Points

- Why did you make the choice you did?
- What is the problem with a little bit of alcohol?
- What if people laugh at you for saying no?
- How would you feel about an uncle or some other trusted adult who offered you alcohol?
- Parents, talk about what it feels like to be drunk—kill the mystery.
- Do you now have a different view on this scenario than you did at the start? Why or why not?
- Would you like to change your answer or stick with it?

The Lord knows how to **rescue the godly from trials** and to hold the unrighteous for punishment on the day of judgment.

(2 Peter 2:9)

Parents, tell your teen this story.

You've liked a boy for a really long time, and he finally asked you out. He's the most popular boy in school and two years older than you. He takes you to a party you'd never have been invited to attend if you weren't with him. Immediately upon arriving at the party, someone shoves a beer into your hand. You try to give it back, but your date wants you to have fun. You don't want to offend him or look like a baby—what do you do?

Now offer the following options with no personal commentary.

Let your teen think about the choices and make an honest decision.

> A. You're horrified that he doesn't know you well enough or doesn't care about you enough to know you don't drink. You ask him to take you home right away.
>
> B. There's no way you're going to risk being a drag. You're totally going to drink that beer.
>
> C. You pretend to sip on the drink, but plan to set it down somewhere when your date isn't looking.
>
> D. You decline the beer, but stay at the party. You aren't responsible for what other people do.

Crucial Step

Use this scenario to guide a discussion about alcohol and parties. Be very careful not to sound judgmental or accusatory. Remember, your teen is exploring thoughts and first impressions—these aren't actual choices . . . yet. If you're realistic about the likelihood that this will happen, you'll be better able to handle it in a rational way.

Discussion Points

- Why did you make the choice you did?
- Have you ever been in a situation like that?
- How common are parties with alcohol among your friends?
- Your convictions are worth more than giving in just to make a boy happy.
- One drink is too many, so don't risk it.
- Reputation is so difficult to build, but so easy to destroy.
- You can always call for a ride home—anytime.
- Do you now have a different view on this scenario than you did at the start? Why or why not?
- Would you like to change your answer or stick with it?

If you belonged to the world, it would love you as its own. As it is, **you do not belong to the world**, but I have chosen you out of the world. That is why **the world hates you**.

(John 15:19)

Parents, tell your teen this story.

You're at a party with a date and you both decide to have some alcohol. You drink a couple of beers and sneak to the back of the house where you start cuddling, then kissing. Things start to get out of control and you feel your resolve slipping out of reach. But you're not even sure you care anymore. The moment feels too good to stop. What do you do?

Now offer the following options with no personal commentary.

Let your teen think about the choices and make an honest decision.

A. What can you do? You're in too deep to backtrack now, so you let things go where they will.

B. You dig deep and fight through the haze of alcohol for the reason you committed to purity. With resolve, you pull yourself out of that situation and call home for a ride.

C. You stop the physical contact and find a friend who says she hasn't been drinking to take you home—you've had too much to drink to drive yourself and your date was drinking too.

D. You manage to stop the physical activity and convince your date to rejoin the party.

Crucial Step

Use this scenario to guide the discussion about the ways alcohol can affect decisions and convictions. Be very careful not to sound judgmental or accusatory. Remember, your teen is exploring thoughts and first impressions—these aren't actual choices . . . yet. Before teens ever begin dating, there should be clear expectations about appropriate levels of physical contact. See *Hot Buttons Dating Edition* for help with these discussions.

Discussion Points

- Why did you make the choice you did?
- Can you ever be 100 percent sure you'd be able to get out of there without things going too far?
- How much alcohol can a person consume and still be safe to drive?
- Parents, reiterate the guidelines for calling home for a ride.
- Establish or review standards and guidelines about both alcohol use and physical contact.
- Do you now have a different view on this scenario than you did at the start? Why or why not?
- Would you like to change your answer or stick with it?

Watch and pray so that you will not fall into temptation. The spirit is willing, but **the flesh is weak**. (Matt. 26:41)

Parents, tell your teen this story.

Your mom and dad or other trusted adult (maybe even a youth leader) has an occasional alcoholic beverage, like a glass of wine with dinner. They tell you it's wrong, but they do it themselves. It's so hypocritical, which is a sin too, just the same as any other. If they're going to be hypocrites, there's no point in listening to what they say. Until now, you've always turned down any offers of alcohol from your friends—it is illegal, after all—but next time . . . What do you do?

Now offer the following options with no personal commentary.

Let your teen think about the choices and make an honest decision.

A. You'll stay true to your instincts and wait until you're older—true friends will be proud of you and may even secretly admire you for my stand.

B. Even though you don't feel quite right about it, you give it a try to see if you like it.

C. Your parents are not *really* against drinking; they're just being overprotective. But you'll be responsible and not drink and drive or ride with others who do.

D. If your parents are going to be hypocrites, they deserve to suffer the consequences. You grab the next drink you're offered.

Crucial Step

Use this scenario to guide a discussion about adults and alcohol compared to teen alcohol use. Be very careful not to sound judgmental or accusatory. Remember, your teen is exploring thoughts and first impressions—these aren't actual choices . . . yet. While D might sound harsh, it is a justification teens use. Consider that as you look at the choices you're modeling and open a discussion about your adult choices.

Discussion Points

- Why did you make the choice you did?
- Discuss the difference between being an adult and being a teen, and how laws and biblical guidelines apply.
- Discuss your feelings about alcohol use for adults.
- What is the law related to teens consuming alcohol?
- Is driving while intoxicated the only concern related to teens (or anyone) and alcohol?
- How can you best honor God at this point in your life?
- What can I do as your parent to help you stick to your commitments?
- Discuss chapter 5.
- Do you now have a different view on this scenario than you did at the start? Why or why not?
- Would you like to change your answer or stick with it?

Let everyone be subject to the governing authorities, for **there is no authority except** that which **God** has established. (Rom. 13:1)

Parents, tell your teen this story.

You were at a friend's house and several of your friends were smoking pot. You didn't want to do it at first, but they teased you and made you feel like an outsider. You decided to try it just once. You took one little puff. It didn't do much to you except make your stomach a little sick. Now you regret that decision because you can't ever take it back; you can't say you've never done drugs. It wasn't worth it, but now they'll always expect you to participate. What can you do?

Now offer the following options with no personal commentary.

Let your teen think about the choices and make an honest decision.

A. You tell your friends that you were wrong for doing drugs and ask them not to pressure you again. If they want to do it, fine—just leave you out of it.

B. You had expected to feel a lot of physical effects from the marijuana, but it didn't do much to you. Maybe you did it wrong. You'll ask a good friend for advice.

C. You won't do it next time, but you don't tell your friends you regret trying it.

D. You vow never to do it again and have a talk with your parents so they can let the other parents know.

Crucial Step

Use this scenario to guide a discussion about the effects of marijuana and the slippery slope toward addiction. Be very careful not to sound judgmental or accusatory. Remember, your teen is exploring thoughts and first impressions—these aren't actual choices . . . yet. Talk openly about the ability Christians have to restore themselves in God's eyes to a pre-sin condition through forgiveness, but that a reputation in people's eyes is difficult to reconstruct.

Discussion Points

- Why did you make the choice you did?
- Forgiveness covers all sins.
- Repentance doesn't just mean you're sorry, it means you turn from the behavior and don't do it again.
- Addiction starts with one step—the friends are on a slippery slope.
- How would you feel if you didn't let your friends' parents know and something bad happened?
- See the resource section for hotlines and information.
- Do you now have a different view on this scenario than you did at the start? Why or why not?
- Would you like to change your answer or stick with it?

We know that **anyone born of God does not continue to sin**; the One who was born of God keeps them safe, and **the evil one cannot harm them**

(1 John 5:18)

Parents, tell your teen this story.

A friend's family is bringing you along on a weekend trip to the beach. You've been looking forward to this for a long time. When it's time to pack up the car to leave, you notice your friend's parents pack some wine coolers. You don't think much of it until you get into the car and smell alcohol in the car. It seems they've already been drinking. If you let them drive after they've been drinking, there could be a lot of trouble, not to mention how dangerous it would be. But if you say something, you won't be able to go with them and you've really been looking forward to it. What do you do?

Now offer the following options with no personal commentary.

Let your teen think about the choices and make an honest decision.

> A. There's no way you'll ride with someone who's been drinking, so you pretend to have a headache and say you'll walk home. There's nothing you can do to stop them from going; they're adults!
>
> B. You refuse to get in the car with them and explain why. You call your parents and ask them for help because your friend's parents seem kind of angry with you.
>
> C. There's hardly any alcohol in a wine cooler, so they probably aren't really drunk and you're not driving that far. You don't want to miss the weekend at the beach, so you ride along with your eyes closed as you pray for safety.
>
> D. It's no big deal. You go along for the trip and hope you and your friend can sneak one of those wine coolers when you get to the beach.

Crucial Step

Use this scenario to begin a discussion about drinking and driving. Be very careful not to sound judgmental or accusatory. Remember, your teen is exploring thoughts and first impressions—these aren't actual choices . . . yet. You need to be realistic about the different choices other families make. You can't trust that everyone shares your values.

Discussion Points

- Why did you make the choice you did?
- You can't know for sure how much people have had to drink or how it's affecting them until it might be too late.
- What are the house rules about getting in the car with someone who has had even one drink?
- Discuss the dangers of drunk driving. Review chapter 5.
- You should never feel pushed to do things you don't want to do or that feel risky to you.
- No amount of fun is worth risking your life.
- You and your friend's family aren't the only people at risk in this scenario.
- Pray that God will protect you from even being in a situation like this.
- Do you now have a different view on this scenario than you did at the start? Why or why not?
- Would you like to change your answer or stick with it?

Be on your guard; stand **firm in the faith**; be courageous; **be strong**. (1 Cor. 16:13)

Parents, tell your teen this story.

You walk into the bathroom after biology class, and you see three people come out of the large stall together. One of them is an old friend who has recently pulled away from you. All three of them are wiping their noses and sniffing. They all make eye contact with you as they step past to leave the restroom. You believe they were in there doing drugs, but you have no real proof. What do you do?

Now offer the following options with no personal commentary.

Let your teen think about the choices and make an honest decision.

A. You have no proof, so there's nothing you can do. You plan to avoid that restroom from now on.

B. Since you know they know you know, you don't want them to worry that you'll be bothered by what they're doing. You let them know it's cool with you that they do whatever they want to do.

C. You're going to take matters into your own hands and have a heart-to-heart with your friend. You can probably get through easier than a parent or teacher.

D. You go right to the office and tell the principal or guidance counselor what you saw.

Crucial Step

Use this scenario to guide a discussion about drug use. Be very careful not to sound judgmental or accusatory. Remember, your teen is exploring thoughts and first impressions—these aren't actual choices . . . yet. Many of these scenarios have to do with the avoidance of personal sin, but your teen also needs to be empowered to take action against others' dangerous behavior.

Discussion Points

- Why did you make the choice you did?
- What would concern you in that situation?
- Could you be friends with someone who does drugs? Why or why not?
- What are some of the consequences of drug use?
- How would you feel if you didn't tell anyone and something bad happened?
- Discuss the importance of involving an adult and not trying to handle it alone.
- Do you now have a different view on this scenario than you did at the start? Why or why not?
- Would you like to change your answer or stick with it?

Do not be overcome with evil, but **overcome evil with good**. (Rom. 12:21)

Parents, tell your teen this story.

You're out shopping with your friends and when you get into the fitting room, one of them opens her purse and pours out a bunch of different things like markers, a bottle of correction fluid, and a little spray can. Each friend grabs something, stuffs it in a baggie and starts sniffing from it. You're shocked because you had no idea they did that sort of thing, but you're kind of intrigued. Someone holds a plastic bag with a Sharpie right under your nose and waits for you to inhale. If you don't, you know they'll make fun of you. What do you do?

Now offer the following options with no personal commentary.

Let your teen think about the choices and make an honest decision.

> A. Push her hand away and tell them you don't do that. If they make fun of you, fine.
>
> B. Go ahead and take a whiff. You've always wondered what it would be like. The high only lasts a minute or two and it's just one time . . .
>
> C. Push her hand away, tell them you don't do that, then tell your parents or an adult what's going on.
>
> D. Take a big whiff and experience the high. When it fades away, you reach for something else to try.

Crucial Step

Use this scenario to begin a discussion about using inhalants. Be very careful not to sound judgmental or accusatory. Remember, your teen is exploring thoughts and first impressions—these aren't actual choices . . . yet. The use of inhalants may have already been presented to your tween or teen. Create a safe environment for this discussion so you can learn the truth.

Discussion Points

- Why did you make the choice you did?
- How curious are you about this sort of thing? Why?
- On a scale of 1 to 10, how serious do you think the use of inhalants really is?
- Should your friends have exposed you to that? What kind of friends do you want to associate with?
- Could you see something like this happening?
- Discuss the dangers as outlined in chapter 6.
- Do you now have a different view on this scenario than you did at the start? Why or why not?
- Would you like to change your answer or stick with it?

Blessed are those who are persecuted because of righteousness, for **theirs is the kingdom of heaven**. (Matt. 5:10)

Parents, tell your teen this story.

Your best friend and her boyfriend drink a lot at parties and even when they're alone. It seems to you like they act different when they're drinking: they talk more sexually and hang all over each other. You and your best friend were together in youth group when you both made a commitment to wait until marriage to have sex. You're getting concerned they'll do something that they'll regret while they're under the influence of alcohol. You've tried talking to your friend about her drinking problem, but she just blows you off. What can you do?

Now offer the following options with no personal commentary.

Let your teen think about the choices and make an honest decision.

> A. You talk to your parents and let them decide how to handle it, knowing they'll probably tell your friend's parents what's been going on.
>
> B. You hope they drink enough that they don't remember whatever it is they might regret doing.
>
> C. You continue to talk to your friend about her drinking and her commitment to purity, but ultimately it's her decision.
>
> D. You talk to your friend again and let her know that if the drinking doesn't stop, you'll have to go to her parents.

Crucial Step

Use this scenario to guide a discussion about how alcohol weakens resolve and makes it easier to give in to temptation. Be very careful not to sound judgmental or accusatory. Remember, your teen is exploring thoughts and first impressions—these aren't actual choices . . . yet. Scenarios that focus on the actions of a friend are a safe way to explore your child's thoughts on various issues.

Discussion Points

- Why did you make the choice you did?
- Discuss chapter 5.
- Make plans for how to avoid tempting situations and how to help your friends out of them.
- The friend might get mad now, but will appreciate your loving concern in the long run.
- If she does something serious like having sex with her boyfriend, you'll regret not doing something about it while you had the chance.
- Ask the friend to compare her commitment to self and God with her desire to party. Is it worth the risk?
- Do you now have a different view on this scenario than you did at the start? Why or why not?
- Would you like to change your answer or stick with it?

A friend loves at all times, and a brother is born for a time of adversity. (Prov. 17:17)

Parents, tell your teen this story.

Everyone does it, right? It's the night of the big party and you and your friends have all had a couple of drinks. The designated driver gets sick and has to go home. He offers you a ride home, but you don't want to leave the party yet. You'll figure out the ride thing later. When later comes, though, you've had more to drink and so have all of your other friends. You're supposed to be home in an hour. How are you going to get home?

Now offer the following options with no personal commentary.

Let your teen think about the choices and make an honest decision.

> A. There aren't many cars out at this time of night anyway, so the chances of an accident are nearly zero. You'll find a ride with someone who's heading in the direction of your house.
>
> B. You'll just suck it up and drive yourself. If you stop drinking now, you'll be fine.
>
> C. You call home for a ride, even though you know you're going to get busted for drinking.
>
> D. You ask if you can just spend the night at the house. That way you won't get caught for drinking and you won't have to worry about driving.

Crucial Step

Use this scenario to guide a discussion about drinking and driving. Be very careful not to sound judgmental or accusatory. Remember, your teen is exploring thoughts and first impressions—these aren't actual choices . . . yet. It's difficult to talk about situations like this since you hope your teen won't choose to drink. Still, resist the urge to deny the possibility, and help your teen make a plan for safety.

Discussion Points
- Why did you make the choice you did?
- It's impossible to go backward. Once the choice is made and an accident happens, it's too late.
- Alcohol is addictive and you can't know your threshold until after addiction takes hold.
- Hang out with friends who make wise choices and avoid alcohol.
- Discuss house rules and safeguards for getting out of a sticky situation.
- Do you now have a different view on this scenario than you did at the start? Why or why not?
- Would you like to change your answer or stick with it?

No temptation has overtaken you except what is common to mankind. And **God is faithful**; he will not let you be tempted beyond what you can bear. But when you are tempted, **he will also provide a way out** so that you can endure it. (1 Cor. 10:13)

Parents, tell your teen this story.

Some of your friends got you to try sniffing permanent markers. At first it seemed like a big joke. What could a marker do to a person, after all? After a few minutes, though, you realized that it gave you an actual high, much like you assumed illegal drugs would do. But they're not illegal. And they're cheap. And no one ever told you not to use them. Since then you've made sure you had one of those big, fat markers with you at all times. You pull it out in the bathroom stalls and take a big whiff whenever you have a moment alone. Lately you've been getting headaches if you wait too long between uses. Does that mean you're addicted? What do you do?

Now offer the following options with no personal commentary.

Let your teen think about the choices and make an honest decision.

> A. You run to the nearest garbage can where you toss out the marker and then go to your parents for help.
>
> B. You stop using them immediately, but you don't tell anyone about it.
>
> C. You have to stop using the markers to get high—and you will . . . soon.
>
> D. You're not hurting anyone, and it hasn't caused you any trouble yet. You don't really see a problem with it. Besides, if you stopped, you'd have to deal with those rotten headaches for who knows how long.

Crucial Step

Use this scenario to guide a discussion about inhalants. Be very careful not to sound judgmental or accusatory. Remember, your teen is exploring thoughts and first impressions—these aren't actual choices . . . yet. Be careful not to minimize the use of inhalants. They should be talked about with the same level of importance as any other drug.

Discussion Points

- Why did you make the choice you did?
- Discuss chapter 6 in detail.
- Parents, discuss what it feels like to be high—kill the mystery.
- Inhalants lead to addiction in the same way as other drugs.
- Inhalants can be even more addictive and dangerous than other drugs; they're poisonous to the body.
- See the resource section for additional tools about addiction.
- Do you now have a different view on this scenario than you did at the start? Why or why not?
- Would you like to change your answer or stick with it?

Confess your sins to each other and **pray for each other** so that you may be healed. **The prayer of a righteous person is powerful** and effective. (James 5:16)

Strategic Scenario 14

Parents, tell your teen this story.

You've been complaining to your best friend that you're feeling really fat. You've noticed some changes in your body and you don't like it at all. She recommends this diet pill that will not only help you take the extra pounds off, but it will help you stay awake in class and focus on everything better. Plus, it's legal. You can buy it right from the drugstore with no problem. She offers you a few to get started. What do you do?

Now offer the following options with no personal commentary.

Let your teen think about the choices and make an honest decision.

A. If it's legal and cheap, why not? You down one.
B. It's worth a try, but first you're going to Google it.
C. You really want to give it a try, but you should talk to your mom or dad about it first.
D. Drugs for weight loss? No way.

Crucial Step

Use this scenario to guide a discussion about the use of over-the-counter medications. Be very careful not to sound judgmental or accusatory. Remember, your teen is exploring thoughts and first impressions—these aren't actual choices . . . yet. This will be an opportunity to guide your teen's early perceptions of OTC drug use.

Discussion Points

- Why did you make the choice you did?
- What's wrong with drugs that are legal and okay for even a teenager to buy from every store?
- Discuss the statistics in chapter 9.
- Is OTC drug use happening around you already?
- Have you ever been tempted to misuse OTC medications or prescription drugs?
- Discuss the consequences and the potential ways to get help.
- Do you now have a different view on this scenario than you did at the start? Why or why not?
- Would you like to change your answer or stick with it?

So whether you eat or drink or whatever you do, **do it all for the glory of God**.
(I Cor. 10:31)

Parents, tell your teen this story.

You tried out for your favorite sport and made the team. Now you have a whole new set of friends and they're all super popular. You're in social heaven! Parties, games, pep rallies—it's what you've always wanted out of high school. The problem is, there are always drugs and alcohol at the parties. Although all the players have to agree to stay clean, no teachers, coaches, or parents seem to even suspect that they're not. You never thought you'd be tempted by those things, but you find yourself seriously considering trying some of them. You really want to be cool and popular more than anything right now. There will be plenty of time to be "good" later. What do you do?

Now offer the following options with no personal commentary.
Let your teen think about the choices and make an honest decision.

A. No. Even though the things of the world—sin—can be appealing sometimes, no amount of popularity is worth doing those things. You'll still go to the parties and hang out, but you'll turn down the drugs and alcohol.

B. You have to try, just once, so the others won't think you're a religious fanatic. After that, they'll leave you alone about it and you'll have it out of your system.

C. You wanted the full experience, so you're going to have it. Parties, drinking, a little drugs now and then, as long as it doesn't get carried away. The other kids do it and they seem to be having a blast, so why not you?

D. Not only do you refuse to cave in to the pressure, but you involve your parents so they can get some help for the teens who are drinking and doing drugs.

Crucial Step

Use this scenario to guide a discussion about drugs and alcohol. Be very careful not to sound judgmental or accusatory. Remember, your teen is exploring thoughts and first impressions—these aren't actual choices . . . yet. The motivation for drug and alcohol use is as important to understand as the effects and dangers.

Discussion Points

- Why did you make the choice you did?
- How important is popularity to you?
- Do you think you'd be at risk of doing something you know is wrong just to be more popular?
- Popularity isn't worth it.
- Discuss chapter 4.
- Addiction is a slippery slope—this is exactly where it starts.
- Check the resources section for information about addiction.
- Do you now have a different view on this scenario than you did at the start? Why or why not?
- Would you like to change your answer or stick with it?

Do not be misled: **"Bad company corrupts good character."** Come back to your senses as you ought, and **stop sinning**; for there are some who are ignorant of God. (1 Cor. 15:33–34)

PART FOUR

Parent-Teen STUDY GUIDE

Congratulations on making it this far through *Hot Buttons Drug Edition*! This book has dealt with some tough issues and walked you through the practice of using Strategic Scenarios to prepare your teens for the issues related to drug and alcohol abuse and addiction. Now we're going to press in a little deeper and do some work on the spiritual side of choices, sin, confession, and forgiveness. No matter the ages of your children, you'll find some common ground and will learn something about each other through these studies.

As lines of communication open, and awareness deepens through the use of the Strategic Scenarios, pray for guidance as to the right time to go through these studies. I hesitate to write a formula that tells you precisely when that is, because each family situation is different. I'd rather leave the timing up to the guidance of the Holy Spirit. But when you do, I recommend that you work through these studies individually, then come together to discuss your findings.

Visit www.hotbuttonsite.com to find a downloadable and printable version of this study guide in which space for writing is included, so everyone can have a copy for personal study.

Confession

chapter 12

Very **truly I tell you**, the one who *believes* has eternal life. (John 6:47)

. . . **Jesus is the Messiah**, the Son of God, and that **by** *believing* you may have life in his name. (John 20:31)

Jesus said to her, "I am the resurrection and the life. The one **who** *believes* **in me will live**, even though they die; and whoever lives by believing in me will never die. Do you *believe* this?" (John 11:25–26)

If you **confess with your mouth Jesus as Lord**, and *believe* **in your heart** that God raised Him from the dead, **you will be saved**; for with the heart a person *believes*, resulting in righteousness, and with the mouth he confesses, resulting in salvation. (Rom. 10:9–10 NASB)

◀ According to these verses, what is required for salvation?

Stop and think. Have you confessed with your mouth and believed in your heart that Jesus is Lord? Share the answer with your study partner(s).

◀ What does that mean to you to have made that choice?

If you haven't done that but would like to now, take a walk through the following Scriptures. If you're a Christian already, it's still a good exercise to look at these foundational truths as a refresher.

◀ Read Romans 3:23. Who has sinned?

◀ Read Romans 6:23a. What is the price of sin?

Sin requires a penalty. The only payment for it is death, blood. Worse than a physical death, though, is the spiritual death that separates us from God for eternity.

◀ Read Romans 6:23b. What is God's gift?

◀ Read Romans 5:8. How much does God love you?

Jesus gave His own life on the cross to pay the penalty for all of our sin. He, an innocent man, took your death sentence and stood in your place, giving you new life in exchange for His death.

◀ Read Romans 10:13 and Revelation 3:20. Who qualifies for salvation?

If you'd like to welcome Jesus into your life and receive the free gift of eternal life that He offers, simply pray this prayer:

> *Dear Jesus, I believe in You. I believe that You are the Son of God and my Savior and Lord. I ask You to forgive my sins and make*

me clean. Please help me do the right thing, but I thank You for the forgiveness You offer me when I mess up. I give my life to You. Amen.

If you took that step, *congratulations*!

Everything pales in comparison to the choice to walk with Jesus through your life. Now we can apply that choice of confession to the issues in this book and to your relationships.

> Therefore **confess your sins** to each other and pray for each other so that you may be healed. The **prayer of a righteous person is powerful** and effective. (James 5:16)

Confessing your sins *to others* is not a requirement of salvation. James 5 doesn't suggest that you should confess your sins to each other so that you might be saved. Confession to God is the only path to salvation. James 5 is referring instead to healing of the mind, the mending of broken trust, and the repairing of damaged relationships that only comes about by seeking forgiveness from those you have wronged in the past.

Confession clears the air and allows forgiveness to blossom where bitterness once festered. And confession carries healing power no matter what the response is. In other words, your confession starts the healing process in you, regardless of how it's received or if forgiveness is immediately granted.

◀ Work together to write a description of the purpose of confession in family relationships.

Though forgiveness in Christ is complete, sin continues to thrive in the darkness of secrecy. Confession to a loved one deflates sin's power like the air rushing out of a balloon. The sin shrivels, its grip releases, and its power dies. What was once a tool of the enemy to destroy you and your family is now a bonding agent that unites and builds strength and character. What a victory!

When is it important to confess to each other?

- When the issue is causing division
- When there is bitterness
- When you're unable to find peace
- When you need forgiveness

Now is the time to take a risk. You've confessed to God, and you're forgiven of your sins because of the death and resurrection of God's Son, Jesus. Now it's time to lay your heart bare before your loved ones. Trust that we'll get to the forgiveness part of this study just as soon as you turn the page. Let go of the fear of admitting your faults. Confess today so you can be forgiven and see your relationships restored once and for all.

Open your heart and mind, and let the Holy Spirit reveal the things that you need to let out. Let this be a safe moment in your family in which you feel free to lay your heart bare and free your spirit of any guilt or condemnation that binds you.

◀ Take this time to confess whatever the Lord is bringing to your mind. You may verbalize your confession, or write it in your own notebook or in your study guide (which you can find at www.hotbuttonsite.com).

Trust that your loved ones' response to your confession will be one of forgiveness—the next chapter will lead you through that.

Parent's Prayer

Father, I confess the times I've failed as a parent and ask You to forgive me and help me have more self-control and wisdom when I respond to things. Please help me to be a godly example and a role model for my kids. Give us the kind of relationship that mirrors the one You have with us. Thank You for Your example of unconditional love, continual acceptance, and constant approachability. Make me that kind of parent, and help my family to forgive me for the times I haven't been. Amen.

Teen's Prayer

Dear God, please forgive me for not respecting my parents all the time. Help me to honor the values we've decided upon as a family and uphold them in all things. Give me the strength to say no when I'm pressured to do all sorts of wrong things. Please help me to be a better son/daughter and make us a loving and united family that serves You together. Amen.

13 Forgiveness

Following belief and confession is forgiveness. Ah, what a blessed state to live in . . . forgiven. The very word elicits a sense of peace and calm. It inspires me to take a deep breath and rest for a moment in gratitude.

How about you? Do you feel forgiven?

> If we **confess our sins**, he is faithful and just and will **forgive us** our sins and **purify us** from all unrighteousness. (1 John 1:9)

Do you believe that you're forgiven? Sometimes it hits like a tsunami as the waves of peace wash over the heart. For others, it's more of a steady rain that takes time to feel. It's okay, either way. Whether you feel forgiven or not, you can have faith that you are, in fact, purified and holy before God.

So God has forgiven you, but now what does He expect you to do about other people who have wronged you?

For if you **forgive other people** when they sin against you, your **heavenly Father will also forgive you**. But if you do not forgive others their sins, your Father will not forgive your sins. (Matt. 6:14–15)

◀ What does that verse teach about forgiveness?

◀ How do you feel about that?

Forgiving others is often a simple act of obedience and a step of faith. If you're angry or wronged in some way, you're rarely going to feel like forgiving those who hurt you. Forgiveness, in that case, is a gift from God planted in your heart so that you might extend it toward those who sinned against you.

Would you be surprised if I told you that offering forgiveness benefits you far more than it benefits the person you're attempting to forgive? Surrendering in that way allows God to work more deeply in your life.

◀ Read Ephesians 4:25 and Luke 15. How do you think God wants us to receive someone's confession?

◀ Now, think about this question: Can you truly accept someone's confession and offer forgiveness without holding on to any bitterness or contempt?

◀ What makes that easy or difficult for you?

◀ Read Matthew 18:21–35. Who do the characters in this parable represent? What is the debt? What is the parable trying to show us?

> **Bear with each another** and forgive one another if any of you has a grievance against someone. **Forgive as the Lord forgave you**. And over all these virtues put on love, which binds them **all together in perfect unity**. (Col. 3:13–14)

Parents, name some times you've been forgiven of things in your life and share them here. Try for at least five examples. Spend as much time thinking about this as necessary.

When you see it written out like that, does it give you a different perspective on your teen's sins?

But I'm not God!

What about when it's just too bad, and I'm truly unable to let go of the anger toward someone?

> And when you stand praying, if you hold anything against anyone, **forgive him**, so that your Father in heaven may forgive you your sins. (Mark 11:25)

> Do not judge, and you will not be judged. Do not condemn, and you will not be condemned. **Forgive**, and you will be forgiven. (Luke 6:37)

Believe me, I get it. It's not easy to forgive those who have committed a painful wrong against you and are truly guilty. The problem is that unforgiveness drives a wedge into our daily walk with God. That free and open walk with a loving Savior becomes strained and even avoided when your spirit knows it's harboring something God cannot abide. He talked to His children about this specific issue because He doesn't want it to divide you from Him.

- Are you able to forgive each other for the things confessed before God in the last chapter? Are you able to treat those confessions with the same manner of grace that God has shown you? Is anything standing in your way? Take turns sharing.

We've made huge progress through confessing to God and each other, receiving God's grace, and forgiving others. I'd like to encourage you to backtrack a little and dig a little deeper.

- What are you still holding on to that needs to be confessed to your family? What sin still makes you cringe when you consider sharing it? Why can't you let it go?

Now's the time to take a chance. Forgiveness is a step away. Families, assure each other that it's safe to unload anything at this time. God has forgiven your sins, past, present, and future—now allow your family to do the same.

Confession followed by forgiveness is a life-changing gift of healing.

Parent's Prayer

Heavenly Father, I'm so grateful for Your grace and forgiveness. I'm so grateful that it extends to cover the mistakes I make as a Christian and as a parent. Please help me forgive others like You have forgiven me so that I can be an extension of Your arm of mercy to those around me. Let me show grace to my children so they will trust me with their sins and their feelings. Help me not to expect them to be perfect, but rather to see them as You see them and readily offer forgiveness at all times. Amen.

Teen's Prayer

Lord, I've done some dumb things—thank You for forgiving me for them. Your gift of salvation has changed my life, and I'm not the same person I was before You came into it. Thank You, too, for helping me and my family work through some of these things. It all makes sense when we talk about it and look at what the Bible says. Help me not to hold grudges against people who have hurt me, and help me to be obedient to You and to my parents. Please help me make good decisions and not to give in to peer pressure. Amen.

Clean Slate

chapter 14

> For as **high as the heavens** are above the earth,
> **so great is his love** for those who fear him;
> as far as the east is from the west,
> so far has he **removed our transgressions** from us.
>
> (Ps. 103:11–12)

◀ In light of Psalm 103:11–12, what does the following quote mean to you?

> "I can forgive, but I cannot forget," is only another way of saying, "I will not forgive." Forgiveness ought to be like a cancelled note, torn in two, and burned up so it can never be shown against one. —Henry Ward Beecher

Confession + Forgiveness = Perfection . . . *right?*

Unfortunately, I think we all know it doesn't quite work that way. The question I receive at this point in the discussion goes something like this:

"So, if I continue to mess up and the people I've forgiven continue to mess up, how can we live with a clean slate?"

◀ Read Romans 7:14–20. What does Paul do? What is he unable to do? Why is he unable to do it?

Paul is a believer. He's forgiven. He's a mighty servant of God, yet he sins. He wants to do what is right, but he often cannot. He doesn't want to do wrong, but often cannot stop himself.

◀ Continue on by reading Romans 7:21–25.

No matter how committed you are to a clean slate, your enemy, the devil, wants nothing more than to sabotage forgiveness, trust, and peace. He is the antithesis of the love you feel for each other and will stop at nothing to erode it.

There are three steps to combat the devil's attacks.

◀ Read James 4:6–8.

Step One: _____ the devil.

What does that mean to you?

What are some ways to do that as it relates to the subject of this book?

◀ Read Luke 6:27 and Acts 7:54–60.

Step Two: _____ your enemies. _____ for those who have mistreated you.

What does that mean to you?

What are some ways to do that as it relates to the issues you've been addressing with the Strategic Scenarios?

◀ Reread James 4:6–8.

Step Three: _____ _____ to God and He will _____ _____ to you.

What does that mean to you?

What are some ways to do that as it relates to the hot-button issues you've been addressing?

Immerse yourself in Scripture and prayer to counter the devil's attacks.

Romans 7 (which we looked at above) ends with a description of the battle between Paul's sin nature and his commitment to God. Good ol' Paul admits that he messes up all the time. But we know that, even though he claimed to be at war with the flesh and struggling with sin, he found favor with God. Let's take a look at Romans 8:1–4 to see the resolution:

> Therefore, **there is now no condemnation** for those who are in Christ Jesus, because through Christ Jesus the law of the Spirit who gives life has **set you free from the law of sin** and death. For what the law was powerless to do because it was weakened by the flesh, God did by **sending his own Son in the likeness of sinful flesh** to be a sin offering. And so he condemned sin in the flesh, in order that the righteous requirement of the law might be fully met in us, who do not live according to the flesh but according to the Spirit.

We have a clean slate before God. It's His promise to us in response to the work of His Son, Jesus. With the slate wiped clean for us, we are able to do the same for others. We're all a work in progress; not a single one of us is perfected and complete. We're complete in Jesus—because of Him—but not because of anything we've done. So allow others the same grace of being "in progress" that your heavenly Father is showing you by keeping your slate free from judgment.

> Being confident of this, that he who **began a good work in you** will carry it on to completion **until the day of Christ Jesus**. (Phil. 1:6)

◀ We looked at Philippians 1:6 back in chapter 3, but let's break it down again. Describe what the phrases in the verse mean to you.

Being confident of this
That He who began
A good work in you
Will carry it on to completion
Until the day of Christ Jesus

◀ How can you apply those truths to yourself and your clean slate before God?

◀ How about others and their slate before you? Is it clean in your eyes? Can you forgive an imperfect person?

From that verse, we're reminded that no one is perfect—we're all a work in progress. Commit to forgiving the failures of others, since you know that you will fail and others will forgive you.

The best way to preempt disappointment is to communicate needs and expectations. Each of you, take a moment to share three needs you have regarding the hot-button issues you've been addressing. For example: "More understanding and space when I'm in a bad mood." I recommend you put this list in writing so there's no confusion later.

Parent Commitments

Speak these commitments out loud to your teen(s):

- I commit to do my best to be a godly example.
- I commit to having an open mind and heart, ready to listen whenever you need to talk.
- I commit to being humble enough to admit when I'm wrong, but strong enough to enforce the boundaries I believe are necessary.
- I commit to _____.
  [fill in the blank based on the needs communicated above]
- I commit to _____.
  [fill in the blank based on the needs communicated above]
- I commit to _____.
  [fill in the blank based on the needs communicated above]

Sign: _____

Date: _____

Remember that your enemy, the devil, seeks to sabotage forgiveness, trust, and peace. It's so easy to stumble down a slippery slope.

The pattern of confession, forgiveness, and a clean slate is perfectly portrayed in the relationship you have with your heavenly Father. He loves you, and wants you to walk in complete forgiveness, confident in His love for you. He also wants you to experience that love in your family.

People fail—they've failed you before, and they'll fail you again. You can't wait for God to perfect those you love, but you can allow His perfect love to cover a multitude of sins—grace from Him to you, and through you to them.

> May God himself, **the God of peace**, sanctify you through and through. May your whole spirit, soul and body **be kept blameless** at the coming of our Lord Jesus Christ. The one who calls you is faithful, and **he will do it**. (1 Thess. 5:23–24)

My Prayer for You

Heavenly Father, I lift this family up to You and thank You for their precious hearts that desire to grow closer together. Please guide them as they join hands and walk together in a united purpose to serve You throughout their lives. Facing these Hot Buttons involves release and trust. Help Mom and Dad to use wisdom in knowing when and how to begin the process of that kind of release, and help the teens to respect the boundaries set by the parents and by Your Word. Give them wisdom and strength when it comes to the choices they must make in life. Grant them Your holy sight to see down the road when the way is unclear to them. Help them also to trust each other with some of the tough decisions. As the years go by, remind them of the things they talked about in this book and the commitments they've made to each other. Give them joy as they embark on life with a clean slate. Amen.

Parent's Prayer

Father, I thank You for my family—they're perfect in Your eyes. Help me to take joy in them each and every day—just like You do. You've given us the gift of a clean slate in Your eyes . . . help us to walk in that freedom with each other too. Help me love my family like You do—unconditionally and unselfishly. Please give me wisdom and patience as I help my teens wade through these years. Amen.

Teen's Prayer

Dear Jesus, thank You for forgiveness and for a clean slate. Thank You for a family who wants to serve You and will work hard to make sure I'm on the right path. Please give me wisdom in all things, especially the choices I have to make about these hot-button issues. Help me to do the right thing and to have the strength to stand up to the pressures of life. Amen.

Recommended Resources

Resources for Improving Communication

Choose HER, Nicole O'Dell and Choose NOW Ministries.
www.choose-her.com
>   Focused on uniting mothers and daughters, offering resources and
>   events.

Girl Talk, Nicole O'Dell and her daughters, Emily and Natalie.
www.choose-now.com
>   Questions from teen readers answered by Nicole and her daughters
>   in the format of their popular blog column.

The Five Love Languages of Teenagers, Gary Chapman.
www.5lovelanguages.com
>   Helps parents assess the specific emotional communication needs
>   of their teen.

Scenarios for Girls Interactive Fiction, Nicole O'Dell.
www.choose-now.com
>   Fiction for tweens that asks the reader to make a moral decision
>   for the main character and learn from the consequences.

Substance Abuse Treatment and Support

Al-Anon-Alateen. www.al-anon.alateen.org
Alateen is for Al-Anon members, usually teenagers, affected by someone else's drinking.

Alcoholics Anonymous World Services. www.aa.org
AA is an organization founded to help people deal with their own alcoholism and/or substance abuse.

Capstone Treatment Center. www.capstonetreatmentcenter.com
A Christian residential treatment program for young men ages fourteen to twenty-four; specializes in drug and alcohol abuse.

Mothers Against Drunk Driving. www.madd.org
MADD exists to create strong social awareness about drunk driving, eliminate underage drinking and driving, and provide support for victims of drunk driving and their families.

National Council on Alcoholism and Drug Dependence. www.ncadd.org
To provide answers regarding alcohol and drug use and dependency, and to connect people with the help they need.

Students Against Drunk Driving. www.sadd.org
To provide students with tools for dealing with underage drinking, drug use, risky and impaired driving, and other destructive decisions.

Teen Challenge International, USA. www.teenchallengeusa.com
Residential treatment facilities for people of all ages dealing with life-controlling addictions.

Recommended Resources

U.S. Department of Health and Human Services' Substance Abuse Mental Health Services Administration (SAMSHA). www.samhsa.gov

SAMHSA works to reduce the effects of alcohol and mental illness on America's communities.

Notes

1. Cited by Drug Rehab Treatment Centers, "What Science Says About Teen Addictions and What It Means for Parents of Teens," accessed May 14, 2012, http://www.drugrehabtreatment.com /what-science-says.html.
2. Megan A. Moreno, Fred Furtner, and Frederick P. Rivara, "Media Influence on Adolescent Alcohol Use," *Pediatrics & Adolescent Medicine* 165, no. 7 (July 2011), http://archpedi.ama-assn.org /cgi/content/short/165/7/680.
3. Roxanne Dryden-Edwards, "Alcohol and Teens," ed. Melissa Conrad Stöppler, MedicineNet.com, last editorial review January 12, 2011, http://www.medicinenet.com/alcohol_and_teens/article.htm.
4. Ibid.
5. Ibid.
6. Statistics from the National Highway Traffic Safety Administration (2010) found in "Underage Drunk Driving Fatalities," The Century Council: Distillers Fighting Drunk Driving and Underage Drinking, accessed May 14, 2012, http://www.centurycouncil .org/sites/default/files/images/AIDF-Rates-Under-21.gif.
7. Michelle Trudeau, "Teen Drinking May Case Irreversible Brain

Damage," January 25, 2010, NPR, http://www.npr.org/templates/story/story.php?storyId=122765890.

8. Quoted in "For Adolescents, Inhalants Are Drug of Choice," Drugs.Com, March 13, 2008, http://www.drugs.com/news/adolescents-inhalants-choice-11347.html. See the NSDUH Report at http://www.oas.samhsa.gov/2k8/inhalants/inhalants.htm.

9. Sharyl Adams and Mary Lib Morgan, "Inhalant Abuse Prevention: Staff Education and Student Curriculum," Commonwealth of Virginia. (2007) Page 7. http://www.doe.virginia.gov/support/prevention/drug_use/inhalant_abuse_prevention.pdf.

10. Join Together staff writer, "New Generation of Teens Abusing Inhalants," The Partnership at Drugfree.org, April 24, 2006, http://www.drugfree.org/join-together/drugs/new-generation-of-teens.

11. "Teen Trend of Huffing Freon Can Freeze Lungs, Cause Brain Damage," by KING 5 HealthLink, KTVB.com, September 25, 2011, http://www.ktvb.com/news/health/130527798.html.

12. Ibid.

13. CADCA (Community Anti-Drug Coalitions of America), "Study Proves Children and Teens Are Using Inhalants to Get High," June 10, 2010, http://www.cadca.org/resources/detail/study-proves-children-and-teens-are-using-inhalants-get-high.

14. US Department of Health and Human Services, "Facts on Prescription and Over-the-Counter Drugs," National Institute on Drug Abuse (NIDA), August 2011, http://teens.drugabuse.gov/peerx/pdf/PEERx_Toolkit_FactSheets_RxDrugs.pdf.

15. Cited in "Prescription Drug Abuse," TeensHealth, The Nemours Foundation, last rev. June 2010, accessed June 5, 2012, http://kidshealth.org

/teen/drug_alcohol/drugs/prescription_drug_abuse.html. See the original CDC "Youth Risk Behavior Surveillance—United States, 2009" at http://www.cdc.gov/mmwr/pdf/ss/ss5905.pdf.

16. "Fact Sheet: Prescription Drug Abuse—a DEA Focus," United States Drug Enforcement Administration, accessed June 5, 2012, http://www.justice.gov/dea/concern/prescription_drug_fact_sheet.html.

17. "Results from the 2008 National Survey on Drug Use and Health: National Findings," SAMHSA Office of Applied Studies, NSDUH Series H-36, HHS Publication No. SMA 09-4434, http://www.oas.samhsa.gov/nsduh/2k8nsduh/2k8Results.cfm.

18. "Generation Rx: A Culture of Pharming Takes Root," Partnership for a Drug-Free America Key Findings of: 2005 Partnership Attitude Tracking Study on Teen Drug Abuse, 2005, http://www.drugfree.org/wp-content/uploads/2011/04/Key-Findings-FINAL1.pdf.

19. "Teen OTC and Prescription Drug Use," Aspen Education Group, 2008, http://www.teenoverthecounterdrugabuse.com/.

20. "OTC Abuse Statistics," TeenHelp.com, accessed June 5, 2012, http://www.teenhelp.com/teen-drug-abuse/OTC-abuse-statistics.html.

21. "Generation Rx: A Culture of Pharming Takes Root."

22. "Trends in the Annual Prevalence of Use of Various Drugs for Eighth, Tenth, and Twelfth Graders," Monitoring the Future Study, Univeristy of Michigan, accessed June 5, 2012, http://www.monitoringthefuture.org/data/07data/pr07t2.pdf.

23. Gigi Stone, "More Teens Abuse Over-the-Counter Drugs," ABC News, December 18, 2005, http://abcnews.go.com/WNT/Health/story?id=1419151#.T8lpzplYv0I.

24. "Over-the-Counter Drug Abuse," Parents, the Anti-Drug, The National

Youth Anti-Drug Media Campaign, access June 5, 2012, http://www
.theantidrug.com/drug-information/otc-prescription-drug-abuse/over
-the-counter-drug-abuse/default.aspx.

25. Cited in "Dependence on Marijuana," University of Washington Alcohol
& Drug Abuse Institute, last updated June 2011, http://adai.washington
.edu/marijuana/factsheets/dependence.htm.

26. John P. Walters, "The Myth of 'Harmless' Marijuana," *Washington Post*,
May 1, 2002, http://www.washingtonpost.com/wp-dyn/content/article
/2002/05/01/AR2006051500683.html.

About the
Author

Youth culture expert **Nicole O'Dell** resides in Paxton, Illinois, with her husband and six children—the youngest of whom are toddler triplets. She's the founder of Choose NOW Ministries, dedicated to battling peer pressure and guiding teens through tough issues while helping parents encourage good decisions, and the host of *Choose NOW Radio: Parent Talk* and *Teen Talk*, where "It's all about choices!" A recent addition to the ministry, Choose HER, focuses on mother-daughter relationships.

A full-time author of both fiction and nonfiction, Nicole's desire is to bridge the gap between parents and teens. Her popular Scenarios for Girls series, the natural segue into the Hot Buttons series, asks teen readers to make tough choices for the main characters and offers alternate endings based on the individual reader's choices.

For more information on Nicole's books or to schedule her for a speaking event or interview, visit www.nicoleodell.com. Follow @Hot_Buttons on Twitter, and like www.facebook.com/HotButtons. Podcasts of *Choose NOW Radio* are available at www.chooseNOWradio.com.